"*The Peacemaker Student Edition* is engaging, concise, practical, and biblically on-target. Ken Sande and Kevin Johnson have done a marvelous job with this book. It has life-changing and freedom-giving potential for young and old alike. I highly recommend it, as I do Peacemaker Ministries."

Randy Alcorn, author, *Heaven*,
The Grace and Truth Paradox,
and *Safely Home*

"Conflict is a part of life. What makes this book so important is that Ken and Kevin understand that resolving conflict is not simply a skill that can be taught. It's how we live out the reality of the gospel in our own lives. Jesus said that the whole of the Old Testament can be summed up in two commands—to love God and to love our neighbor. This book will help students understand what to do and how, through the power of God's Holy Spirit, to do it."

Bob Lepine, cohost, *FamilyLife Today*

"Having seen the effectiveness of peacemaker training in my church, I am excited to recommend this student edition. This should be a must read for all students. It is practical, clear, insightful, and motivating as well as scriptural. Not only does this book teach God's way of handling conflict, but it is useful in building confidence and leadership by example."

Joel C. Hunter, senior pastor, Northland—
A Church Distributed, Orlando, Florida

"*The Peacemaker Student Edition* is an excellent, biblically sound book that provides age-appropriate peacemaking illustrations for youth. I highly recommend it as a resource to teach high school students principles of biblical peacemaking that can be used throughout their lives."

Tony Evans, senior pastor,
Oak Cliff Bible Fellowship;
president, The Urban Alternative

"Ken and Kevin rightly call this the 'student edition,' and their wisdom will help young adults who are still in school. But we're all 'students' in the deeper sense. The biblical word for it is *disciple*. And though my student days lay far in the past, this book taught and retaught me many things essential to living well."

David Powlison, author, *Speaking Truth in Love*;
editor, *The Journal of Biblical Counseling*

THE PEACEMAKER

student edition

Handling Conflict without Fighting Back or Running Away

KEN SANDE

and Kevin Johnson

BakerBooks

a division of Baker Publishing Group
Grand Rapids, Michigan

© 2008 by Peacemaker Ministries

Published by Baker Books
a division of Baker Publishing Group
P.O. Box 6287, Grand Rapids, MI 49516-6287
www.bakerbooks.com

Printed in the United States of America

Library of Congress Cataloging-in-Publication Data
Sande, Ken.
    The peacemaker student edition : handling conflict without fighting back or running away / Ken Sande and Kevin Johnson.
        p.   cm.
    Includes bibliographical references.
    ISBN 978-0-8010-4535-6 (pbk.)
    1. High school students—Religious life. 2. Conflict management—Religious aspects—Christianity. 3. Interpersonal relations—Religious aspects—Christianity. 4. Peace—Religious aspects—Christianity. I. Johnson, Kevin (Kevin Walter). II. Title.
    BV4531.3.S25 2008
    248.8′3—dc22   2007052065

14   15   8   7   6

CONTENTS

INTRODUCTION

God invites you to be a peacemaker. In fact, he wants you and every Christian alive to master his way of handling conflict.

For most of my adult life I (Ken) have been a lawyer and full-time Christian mediator, a specialist in bringing peace to every kind of conflict, from personal lawsuits and business disputes to family issues like divorce and custody battles. I have intervened in neighborhood feuds, church splits, and friend-on-friend fights.

Because you're a breathing human being, you know what conflict feels like at home and school, between friends and strangers. You also know its devastating results. Whenever people lock horns, relationships can be seriously wounded. Conflicts steal time, energy, money, and opportunities for better things. When Christians are fighting, our battles overshadow anything we try to tell the world about Jesus.

In a world full of pain, God wants to involve you in spreading peace. This book will outfit you with a four-step process for handling all kinds of clashes. We call it "The Four G's of Peacemaking":

G1: *Glorify God.*
How can I honor God in this situation?

G2: *Get the log out of your eye.*
How can I own my part of this conflict?

G3: *Gently restore.*
How can I help others own their contribution to this clash?

G4: *Go and be reconciled.*
How can I pass along God's forgiveness and help reach a reasonable solution?

I'm a husband and a dad, a boss and a Christian. In every area of life I have seen these steps turn maddening conflicts into opportunities to grow closer to both people and God. Because I know the Bible's plan for peacemaking, conflict doesn't scare me. In fact, the barriers others consider most overwhelming I see as some of life's most interesting moments. I aim to meet every conflict head-on and as nothing less than an opportunity to glorify God, serve others, and grow to be like Christ.

That outlook might seem risky, if not death-defyingly stupid. But if you're willing to let God train you to be a peacemaker, you can learn responses to conflict that will work in every situation in your real life. You will discover

- When you should overlook mistreatment
- How to admit wrongs
- When to defend your rights
- How to correct others
- When to forgive
- How to strike fair bargains
- What you can do with unreasonable people

- How you can use conflict to showcase God's love and power

The principles you will learn apply to every part of your life; and to help you make all of this practical, key points are reinforced with real-life illustrations. The names of the people involved and unique facts about their stories have been changed to protect the innocent—and the guilty. We have also included at the end of the book some questions for you to think about and discuss with others. Use these to help you learn and see how what we are talking about applies to your own life.

Peacemaking is a daring act of obedience to God. Learning these skills won't lead you to a fairy-tale world of perfect relationships. Yet we promise that you will discover how to do relationships right and enjoy friendships unmatched anywhere else. And once you have experienced that, you won't want to settle for anything less.

G1: GLORIFY GOD

So whether you eat or drink or whatever you do, do it all for the glory of God.

1 Corinthians 10:31

After weeks of watching students come and go from a locker a few feet from hers, Alyssa did what her school's assistant principal had coached everyone to do in freshman orientation. She texted the locker number to the office. Within an hour the school's police liaison found a stash of weed. Alyssa received the promised fifty-dollar reward, and the student caught with drugs was fast-tracked to a one-year expulsion.

Alyssa didn't care about the cash. She reported the student because she hadn't felt safe. Yet when other students concluded she was the one who had "quick-fiftied" her classmate, she was openly threatened.

For Alyssa, doing the right thing turned out all wrong. Pleasing adults infuriated her peers. Solving one conflict created a raft of others. Doing what she was supposed to do didn't work.

You Can't Dodge Conflict

Conflict is unavoidable, but maybe you have picked up the idea that being a good person will help you steer clear of life's major clashes. People won't bug you. Or disrespect you. Or set out to destroy you. Or maybe you have been taught that if you do run afoul of others, turning to God for help will instantly and automatically make everything better.

There's no doubt that God makes you wise so you can avoid plunging headfirst into unnecessary disasters. And the Bible promises that God truly cares about what plagues you. Despite these rock-solid truths, no life is trouble-free. Conflict, in fact, is a certainty of life that you can't escape.

Whatever clashes you face, you *can* count on God for solutions for getting along—ways to deal with everyone from your best friends to your most terrifying foes. Still, you need more than half-truths and guesses about how his plan works. You need his whole story on dealing with people. That's what this book is about. It offers wisdom on how you can give every relationship in your life an entirely different outlook.

You Can Choose to Glorify God

Something significant happens when you decide to follow God's instructions for relationships, especially his insights on conflict. When you focus on him and his ways, you do more than cope. When you choose to study and act on God's plans in every area of your existence, you're living for his glory. It's what the apostle Paul meant when he wrote, "Whatever you do, do it all for the glory of God" (1 Cor. 10:31).

Glory is a biblical word for the essence of God. To "glorify God" means you bring attention to, display, and reveal his perfection. You point with your own life to the enormity of his wisdom, power, and compassion.

When you glorify God by doing relationships according to his plan, you're allowing God to reign in your life. You're enjoying a powerful connection that alters your whole life. And it's all far more than personal. You're also giving everyone around you a reason to respect and praise God's fame.

Picture God's glory as something concrete—an amazing car, for instance. Not some junker like the ones that litter high school parking lots everywhere but something one-of-a-kind exotic. That car is no less glorious if you keep it in the garage. Its perfection doesn't change. But as long as you keep it sheltered, you and your world miss out.

Truth is, if you owned that dream vehicle, you would constantly scan for venues to let everyone see it. To get it out. To let people ogle every millimeter of screaming color, glass, and rubber.

So maybe you would roll it out of the garage and park it in your driveway. That would be a start.

But your car is meant for even more than that. For all anyone knows, it's just a metal shell with no engine. That car is designed for action. As long as it stays parked, you won't experience the joy of driving a perfect machine. Only when you shift into drive can you feel its tires grip winding canyon roads. Or hear its engine hum through mountain switchbacks. Or get the rush of flooring it over the flatlands—within the posted speed limit, of course. But as long as that vehicle sits still, no one can catch sight of its true greatness.

God's glory is far more significant than the most spectacular racer, coupe, or truck you could ever own, and only when you act on God's truth is it fully on display. Glorifying God is an opportunity not for you to parade your own splendor but for you to showcase your amazing Master.

When you live according to God's insights, you enter into the best kind of life he has planned for you. He teaches you how to plot a course through life's most challenging circumstances. No matter what you face, you can choose a radical stance: glorifying God in everything you do.

Your Amazing Opportunity

His master replied, "Well done, good and faithful servant!"

Matthew 25:21

It's not tough to spot conflict in the world. Conflict invades every part of life—even *your* life:

- You clash with a friend who has incredibly strong opinions. You try hard to see her point, but she doesn't care much about yours.
- You resent the coach who sidelines you for a missed play. You want to mouth off, but you also want to keep your spot on the team.
- You have a sibling so unlike you that you wonder how you were born to the same parents. The hurts between you are the thickest walls in the house.

- You're trapped in a running feud with a peer, bickering to prove who is better, stronger, or smarter.
- Your parents set boundaries you don't think you need. They say "safe"; you say "overprotective."
- You rage inside at a boss who manipulates you to work long, late hours you can't handle.
- You get caught in the crossfire of racial battles in your school or neighborhood.
- You're baffled by a teacher famous for confusing lectures. When you ask for help, you get treated like you're the idiot.

You might conclude that every clash is bad, a threat that will inevitably leave you damaged. Or you might view conflict as an obstacle to smash through, even if you injure others in the process. But what if you looked at conflict with a radically different perspective? What if you thought of it as an opportunity to demonstrate respect for God and win benefits for everyone involved?

Human beings deal with conflict in three ways. You can:

- *Fake peace.* You escape, making things look good by pasting on a smile and shrugging that you're okay.
- *Break peace.* You attack, tearing up relationships to get what you want.
- *Make peace.* You work it out, aiming to resolve clashes by searching out solutions that create real justice and authentic harmony.

You can picture these responses to conflict as a curve, like a hill. On the left slope are *peacefaking* (or *escape*) responses to conflict. On the right side are *peacebreaking* (or *attack*) responses. In the center are *peacemaking* (or *work-it-out*) responses.

THE SLIPPERY SLOPE

PEACEBREAKING ZONE
You Attack

- MURDER
- FIGHTING
- GOSSIP
- INSULTS

PEACEMAKING ZONE
You Work It Out

- ACCOUNTABILITY
- GET HELP
- TALK
- OVERLOOK

PEACEFAKING ZONE
You Escape

- DENIAL
- BLAMING
- FLIGHT
- SUICIDE

In every conflict you face, your response plants you somewhere on that hill. But imagine it's slick with ice, so that moving too far from the center sends you skidding—maybe left, maybe right. The farther you go, the easier it is to lose your footing and fall into more extreme reactions. Understanding this slippery slope can help you spot broken ways you might deal with conflict.

Broken Way #1: Peacefaking

Living in the peacefaking zone means you choose tactics to make things feel okay even when they're not.

It starts with *denial*, pretending conflict doesn't exist. If you're any good at acting, your smiles can fool people— maybe even yourself. While denial smoothes a situation for a while, it's no permanent fix.

Picture the next step in peacefaking: *blaming.* You admit there's a problem, yet you attempt to escape by pointing the finger at others. Whenever you cover your tracks, falsely claim innocence, or lie about your contribution to the problem, you're playing the blame game.

Flight is another way of escape. You might cut off a friend or slam the door on a boyfriend or girlfriend. Or you ditch a job or quit an activity. At times you have a legitimate reason to flee, like taking a break to cool off or to escape real danger (more on that in chapter 7). But most of the time your exit just delays a real solution.

People who are impossibly calm, agreeable, and sweet often aren't what they seem. They might just be squirming out of conflict by faking peace. Take this extreme example: In middle school Jesse won praise for overcoming a learning disability to earn Bs and Cs, but by high school he fell behind. When peers mocked his troubles, he cracked jokes about himself. Failing school wasn't his only issue. He never told anyone about his parents' constant battles

Peacefaking in the Bible

- *Denial.* Look at 1 Samuel 2:22–25 for an account of a dad ignoring his sons' sleazy behavior.
- *Blaming.* Adam and Eve try to dodge responsibility in Genesis 3:12–13.
- *Flight.* See Genesis 16:6–8 for an obvious example of running from conflict.
- *Suicide.* In 1 Samuel 31:4 the wounded king Saul kills himself to escape capture by his enemies.

at home or that their divorce was why he suddenly left town. One morning a few months after the move, Jesse's mom found him dead in his bedroom. From the outside Jesse had looked fine, but he had walled himself up in his pain.

When people lose all hope of resolving conflict, they sometimes take that deadly leap: *suicide.* Maybe escaping your problems by ending your life has never entered your mind, but too many of your peers see peace as totally out of reach. According to the U.S. Centers for Disease Control and Prevention, suicide has rocketed to the third leading cause of death among adolescents.[1]

Denial, blaming, flight, and suicide are all peacefaking—pretending there is tranquility when there isn't.

Broken Way #2: Peacebreaking

On the opposite end of the slippery slope is peacebreaking, an attempt to make a situation go your way at all costs. Unless you walk through life with your eyes shut and your ears plugged, you witness a multitude of these attack responses each day.

Slams are when you use humor or sarcasm to clobber people from the side or when you aim insults and other

Peacebreaking in the Bible

- *Insults*. See Nehemiah 4:1–3 for putdowns that come off as both fierce and ridiculous.
- *Gossip*. Check Proverbs 16:28 for the result of back-biting.
- *Fighting*. John 18:10 shows a violent reaction to conflict.
- *Murder*. In Acts 6:8–15 a group of religious rulers silence Stephen, an early church leader, by stoning him to death.

vicious words straight at your opponents. Excusing yourself by saying "I didn't mean it" or "I was just joking" doesn't undo the damage you cause.

Gossip is when you speak those cutting words behind people's backs. Granted, sometimes you need input from others on how to handle a clash. But there's a huge difference between searching out wisdom and backstabbing.

Words obviously aren't the only way people break peace. Know anyone who plays mind games, bullying through manipulation and intimidation? Or people who talk with their fists or other violent acts? All of those attempts to resolve conflict by force can be lumped together as *fighting*.

In the extreme, peacebreaking ends in *murder*. You don't have to catch much news to realize that murder happens everywhere, even close to home. The FBI reports that for every one hundred thousand people, there are five or six killings each year. Even so, murder probably feels distant. Unreal. Jesus, however, said that hatred toward another human is a close cousin of actual murder (see Matt. 5:21–22).

Going into attack mode isn't just a guy thing. Peacebreaking happens whenever people care less about a relationship than about winning an argument, asserting their rights, or getting what they want.

Leaving Broken Ways

Peacemakers see all of the peacefaking and peacebreaking that surrounds them and want to carve a better path through life. They recognize that they need to put an end to the status quo and leave broken ways behind.

Cassie, a high school junior, had always controlled her peers with biting words and harsh glances. She acted like life was one giant parade thrown in her honor, and no one had ever dared to challenge her by telling her to her face that they felt put down and manipulated.

One afternoon Cassie was transporting a load of friends in her family's SUV. When another driver wouldn't let her merge into traffic, she didn't back off. She gunned the engine, then swerved into the lane inches ahead of the other vehicle's bumper. The maneuver sent her SUV skidding sideways. Her vehicle flipped, tumbled off the road, and landed upside down in a ditch.

Although Cassie walked away from the accident, a couple of her passengers spent days recovering in the hospital. Her crowd didn't hide what they thought of Cassie. They poured out phrases like "What were you thinking?" and "You're so incredibly selfish!" and "You're always like this!"

Cassie had to face the real consequences of her combative, peacebreaking lifestyle. Her friends finally shook loose from their peacefaking. It took the accident to jolt all of them into understanding that they needed to speak up sooner about destructive behavior.

Peacemaking—a Better Way

Anyone can fake peace. Or break peace. It takes no imagination at all to plot a quick escape or a brutal attack when you find yourself in a painful conflict. But only by working at peace do you have any chance of finding true justice and genuine harmony. Making peace is also your best shot at keeping conflict from spinning out of control.

Remember? The *peacefaker-peacemaker-peacebreaker* hill is solid ice. Go too far to the left or right, and you shoot down the slippery slope.

That's exactly how conflict works. You lose your grip, then start the slide. The farther you go, the faster you hurtle downward. The more extreme your response, the greater your losses in time, friendships, work, money, or a clean conscience. The farthest ends can even result in death.

Even when peacefaking and peacebreaking don't result in suicide or murder, there's still a problem: neither response solves your issue. The trouble rarely stops. Peacefaking and peacebreaking always result in shattered connections.

That's not all. For Christians, peacefaking and peacebreaking wreak havoc in the worst of ways: they trash your ability to showcase Christ. Whether you're cut off by coldness or sweating it out in hot battle, no one pays attention when you try to tell them about the love of Jesus. Picture Cassie, for example, crashing that SUV and then going to the hospital to pray for her injured friends. No one will tolerate that—unless, that is, she engages in peacemaking to repair the relationship.

The Core of Conflict

Do you want to prevent the problems that result from faking or breaking peace? You can start by exploring what the Bible says about what conflict is and how to deal with it. Peacemaking doesn't come naturally to anyone. Yet God tells us in his Word why clashes occur. And he explains how his gracious love powers your efforts to work out conflicts. The more you understand and obey what God teaches, the more effectively you can settle your disagreements.

You start by understanding what conflict is:

Conflict is a difference in opinion or purpose that frustrates your goals or desires—or someone else's.

That definition covers everything from little disagreements to big blowups to hurt feelings to damaged property. Don't miss the underlying point: conflict happens when you are at odds with another person over what you think, want, or do.

Good Conflict, Bad Conflict

Conflict isn't always bad. The Bible teaches that some differences are natural. Good. Rooted in our God-given individuality. So human beings are bound to have varying opinions, convictions, desires, perspectives, and priorities. Many differences aren't about right or wrong; they are simply the result of personal preferences. If we handle disagreements well, they stimulate dialogue, creativity, and change. They keep life interesting!

You don't have to scan far in the Bible to see that even Christian leaders experienced conflict and came out better for it. In Acts 15:36–41 the great apostle Paul had such a sharp disagreement with his preaching partner, Barnabas, that they split up. Paul didn't think a junior partner, Mark, was mature enough to do ministry. So Paul picked a new sidekick, Silas, and headed for Lystra. Barnabas and Mark went to Cyprus. That clash sounds regrettable until you realize that their solution effectively doubled their missionary output. By going to Lystra, Paul also met his dear friend Timothy. And later Paul came to call Mark his fellow worker (see Philemon 24) and useful helper (see 2 Tim. 4:11). Conflict, handled well, became beneficial.

Trust—and Act

It's normal to see conflict as a hassle or a chance to make others do what you want. But conflict is actually a phenomenal

23

opportunity to demonstrate God's love and power. Gaining real skills in turning a tense situation into something good starts with choosing to handle conflict God's way.

That takes trust. It's counting on God's care for you. It's relying on his accurate understanding of a complex situation. Trust also means you look to God for strength to follow his ways, even when they're the exact opposite of what you feel like doing. You can spot all of these truths wrapped together in Proverbs 3:5–6: "Trust in the LORD with all your heart and lean not on your own understanding; in all your ways acknowledge him, and he will make your paths straight." When you believe that God looks out for you, you can quit fearing what others might do to hurt you.

Real trust in God is no abstract thought or warm feeling. Trust in the Lord empowers you to choose to act in obedience to his commands. You live by his sure instructions, demonstrating unwavering confidence that his ways are your best possible pick. Every time you imitate the humility, mercy, and forgiveness of Jesus, you show your world the awe-inspiring Lord you follow.

Benefiting Others

When you decide to solve conflict God's way, something astonishing happens. Instead of thinking only of yourself, you seize opportunities to serve others. The result is that you benefit them in ways you never imagined.

Serving might not look like what you expect. You can meet spiritual, emotional, or material needs. You might tell them about Jesus or just model how others should act in that situation. You could even help others spot where they have done wrong and need to change.

Suppose you're watching how a friend gets along—or doesn't—with his family at home. You see him sinking fast. Not long ago he would occasionally sass his parents. Now he openly rebels against their every instruction. You might think a supportive friend should shut up and give the guy his space. But you have an opportunity to intervene in the situation. That's the word in Galatians 6:1: "Brothers, if someone is caught in a sin, you who are spiritual should restore him gently." Helping your friend wake up and understand the mess he is causing benefits him far more than your silence.

Imagine how you would impact your world if you saw conflict as a chance to serve others just as Jesus has served you. To the world around you, caring for others sounds absurd. But Jesus commanded you to stretch: "Love your enemies, do good to those who hate you, bless those who curse you, pray for those who mistreat you" (Luke 6:27–28).

Growing to Be Like Christ

There's a more personal payoff to solving conflict God's way: you jump into a process that causes you to grow to be like Christ. Maybe you know that from the day you first believed in Jesus, God began working in you. His job won't be done until the day your life expires. And here's the thing: conflict is one of the premier ways he helps you develop a greater resemblance to Jesus.

Conflict reminds you of your weaknesses and compels you to depend on him. It helps you to practice new, Jesus-like attitudes and habits. Just like working out promotes new muscle growth, the daily exercise of following Jesus strengthens you from the inside out. With the right outlook, you stop worrying about exiting a conflict and start enjoying the fact that God is at work in you.

Back in high school I (Kevin) seemed like a nice enough guy. But when others annoyed me, I used words to slice and stab. Much of my talk with friends was nonstop sarcastic reviews of everyone and everything in sight. When I spent a summer in South America on a mission trip with three dozen new friends from all over the country, I had to find better ways to deal with conflict. Doing two weeks of trip training in a swamp, sharing tents for much of the summer, and baking in the sun as we laid concrete blocks gave me endless opportunities to choose a better way.

I didn't realize how much I had changed until I got back home. A girl I had grown up with asked me why I was so different. She specifically noticed that I didn't trash-talk people anymore. I had only one answer: I was as surprised as anyone that God had changed me.

Your Honored Place

There's one more amazing fact about dealing with clashes God's way: *in every conflict situation, God gives you the opportunity to act as his on-the-ground representative.* He wants you to talk and act as he would—watching out for his goals, displaying his right way of doing things, creatively working toward real peace by maximizing the abilities and spiritual resources he has put in you. If you do that, you're acting as God's steward—an honored person trusted to safeguard a master's treasure (see Luke 12:42). When the Lord examines your work, he wants to be able to say, "Well done, good and faithful servant!" (Matt. 25:21).

This might sound too over-the-top idealistic to work in real life. But you really have only three alternatives. You can be a peacefaker, burying problems until they rise again to bury you. You can be a peacebreaker, dealing harshly with your opponents until you have no one left who dares to call you friend. Or you can become a peacemaker, growing in your ability to deal confidently and effectively with every kind of clash—finding God's way of handling conflict, an approach that truly works.

It's your choice.

Real Peace

If it is possible, as far as it depends on you, live at
peace with everyone.

Romans 12:18

Imagine if we could all hold in our hands the emotional
contents of our hearts. Who knows what these contents
would look like. Maybe sketches that capture certain emotions. Or big orbs glowing with color—red for anger, yellow
for mellow, pink for happy. Or tangible symbols like a bowl
of tears . . . a photograph of a warm embrace . . . a water-
colored landscape of sadness. Whatever we held, we could
look at each other and know immediately how a person was
feeling inside.

What emotions would we encounter? We might see happiness, anticipation, or celebration. There's a good chance,
however, we would see some discouragement. Jealousy. Rage.
Apathy. Fear. Grief. Cynicism. Loss. Weariness.

What would you be holding? What emotions would people see in you?

God intends to fill your heart with a life-altering peace that overflows from you to countless people around you. In a world filled with every variety of pain, you might be the only person bringing peace to those around you.

God's peace is a gift to you. Offering his peace to others isn't just an opportunity. As a believer, it's your responsibility. Yet you are far more likely to want his peace and pass it on if you first understand exactly what it is and how much it matters.

Discovering Peace

Over the past twenty years I (Kevin) have pastored hundreds and hundreds of students. I see parents eye their every move. Teachers measure their intelligence. Coaches clock their speed and analyze their stats. Friends mimic their quirks, and enemies jump on their faults. Yet the fact that there's a world of watching eyes doesn't guarantee that anyone truly knows them.

Of course, no human being can ever completely see what goes on inside you. Ultimately, only you can get honest about what rules your heart, whether it's God and his all-out peace or something else. You know how much of God's peace you have, where you are shaky, and how ready you are to share.

Maybe you worry whether God actually loves you enough to forgive bad things you have done and to help you build fresh habits. Without that question settled, you will cringe when you talk to God—or you will avoid him altogether. Or you might aim your harshest criticisms at yourself, feeling disgust for what you are or aren't. Until you have peace with God, the pain will never be soothed, and you will never run out of reasons to beat yourself up.

The Lord wants to lead you into whatever kind of peace you lack. He wants peace to fill every corner of your heart.

Your God of Peace

If you had to pick one word to describe God, you might choose *love*. After all, the Bible says loudly that "God is love" (1 John 4:8).

Another quality of God is equally significant in the Bible: *peace*. It's so much a part of God's character that he is often called "the God of peace" (as in 1 Thess. 5:23 and Heb. 13:20). His peace is a major gift to his followers, which is why over and over God tells his people to pursue peace and promises to bless those who do. Nearly every New Testament letter starts or ends with a prayer for peace. God even taught his people to say "peace" as a greeting and a good-bye (see Luke 24:36).

Nowhere do you see peace so front and center as in the life of Jesus. From his birth to his world-shaking words and deeds through his crucifixion and resurrection, Jesus radiated peace. Hundreds of years before his birth, Jesus was lauded as the "Prince of Peace" (Isa. 9:6). He came to earth to "guide our feet into the path of peace" (Luke 1:79). When angels hung over his Bethlehem birthplace, they shouted, "Glory to God in the highest, and on earth peace" (Luke 2:14). The more you study the life of Jesus, the more you see that he preached peace. He acted for peace. As history's supreme peacemaker, he sacrificed his life so the world could experience peace with God and each other, now and forever.

3-D Peace

We all hunger for a peace that can be in scarce supply. But if we look to God for what we lack, he never disappoints.

He offers peace in three dimensions—peace with him, with others, and with ourselves.

Peace with God

Peace with God is the core of what it means to be a Christian. But that peace doesn't come about automatically. It's a gift each of us needs to receive.

Experiencing peace with God actually starts by accepting some bad news: not one of us lives a perfect life. Each of us falls short of God's standards. As a result, we find ourselves living far from God. The separation our sin causes runs so deep that the Bible calls it spiritual death: "When someone sins, he earns what sin pays—death" (Rom. 6:23 NCV).

That's the awful truth, but it's only half the story. The amazing news is that God made possible an escape from death. "God so loved the world that he gave his one and only Son, that whoever believes in him shall not perish but have eternal life" (John 3:16). Believing in Jesus means more than going to church or trying hard to be a good person. Those activities won't erase the sins you did yesterday. Or the ones you do today. Or the wrongs you will commit tomorrow.

When you believe in Jesus, you own up to what you are. You admit to being a sinner. You recognize that no number of good deeds can score you God's approval. And you trust that when Jesus hung on the cross, he served the full sentence for your sins, dying the death you deserve.

Even if you know that good news, you might not realize what it has to do with peace. The apostle Paul explains what Jesus accomplished: "Through him God reconciled everything to himself. He made peace with everything in heaven and on earth by means of Christ's blood on the cross" (Col. 1:19–20 NLT). Paul also explains, "Since we have been made right in God's sight by faith, we have peace with God because of what Jesus Christ our Lord has done for us" (Rom. 5:1 NLT).

Peace with People

Jesus's death on the cross doesn't just clear the air between you and God. It also blows away every obstacle to peace between you and other people. You can experience not just an absence of conflict but real mind-to-mind and heart-to-heart connection with others, especially other Christians. That closeness is such a beneficial thing that Psalm 133:1 declares, "It is good and pleasant when God's people live together in peace!" (NCV). It's like when you connect with a friend over coffee or a Coke. Or you head out for a weekend with friends and just sit and talk and talk way into the night. The next thing you know you glance at your watch and two hours have flown by. That's just one example of peace between people, and it's the kind of peace that God wants his followers to enjoy with one another. The rest of this book shows you how to achieve peace when conflict disrupts your relationships with others.

Peace with Yourself

Strength. Wholeness. Contentment. Stability. Rest. Security. Most people never catch that kind of internal calm. Yet it's something you can experience.

Authentic peace depends on a couple of other things happening. You get peace inside when you stay connected to God, putting all your confidence in him: "You will keep in perfect peace him whose mind is steadfast, because he trusts in you" (Isa. 26:3). Moreover, you get peace when you do right toward people, obeying God's instructions: "If only you had paid attention to my commands, your peace would have been like a river, your righteousness like the waves of the sea" (Isa. 48:18).

Suppose you want to ride some of those "waves of the sea." Neither of us lives anywhere near an ocean, though Kevin and his wife spent their first three years of marriage in Los

Angeles. But we both understand that to catch waves you have to do a couple things. You have to get to a beach and then paddle into the water. As long as you stay put far from water, the best you can do is pretend to surf.

It's the same way with experiencing authentic inner peace. It's impossible to find calm if you fail to pursue both peace with God and peace with others. You first need to be reconciled with God by trusting what Jesus did for you on the cross. Then, relying on God's power, you steadily learn to live out his desires for his people. Only then will you find peace with yourself.

Getting God's Unity

Peace with God . . . people . . . yourself. People hunger for all those things. Even those who claim they don't care about connecting with God or others still care deeply about their own inner calm.

In a world that spills over with every kind of pain, being a peacemaker can feel like a lonely business. But it's not your job alone. In fact, people only see peace at its fullest when God's people live peacefully with each other. In the New Testament that kind of person-to-person peace is called "unity."

Unity takes peace beyond you. It's how you prove to the world that Christ and the peace he claims to bring are undeniably real, because when your relationships with others display unity, people see God alive in you. As long as unresolved conflicts and broken relationships dominate you, you can't expect anyone to believe what you say about your amazing life as a Christian.

Right before soldiers arrested Jesus and took him away to the cross, he prayed for himself. Then he prayed for his disciples. Not just for the twelve guys and others who had gathered around him. He prayed for believers in all times and places who would follow him. It's awesome to think that he was praying for you and each one of your Christian friends. Look at what he asked for:

> My prayer is not for [my disciples] alone. I pray also for those who will believe in me through their message, that all of them *may be one*, Father, just as you are in me and I am in you. May they also be in us so that the world may believe that you have sent me. I have given them the glory that you gave me, that they *may be one as we are one*: I in them and you in me. *May they be brought to complete unity to let the world know that you sent me and have loved them even as you have loved me.*
>
> John 17:20–23, emphasis added

You can be sure that as Jesus headed to the cross, he was highly focused in his prayers to his Father. In his final words, he zeroed in on one thought that he judged to be of utmost importance for everyone who would ever believe in him. He didn't pray that his followers would always be happy, that they would always dodge suffering, or that they would always get a fair shake. He prayed that his followers would get along.

Unity is so important to Jesus that he hangs his whole reputation on you and other Christians working together. If unity is that major in his mind, it's something we can't ignore.

The Upshot of Unity

When Christians don't get along, people suffer.

Kayla and Bethany were part of a youth group famed throughout their area for its annual mission trips. Though the girls had known each other since their days toddling around the church nursery, they rarely agreed on anything. As both rose to leadership in the group, their clashes intensified.

When they were asked to pick a location for their final trip before high school graduation, hostilities broke out. Kayla advocated for a nearby project where the group could build long-lasting relationships. Bethany argued for a locale that was more exotic, more inspiring—and more expensive. The girls took stabs at each other's spiritual commitment and pressed friends to choose sides.

Everyone felt the squeeze. Core students were turned off by the arguing. Fringe students wandered away—some to other churches, some to nowhere. News of the battle even spread to school. While the girls' classmates didn't get all the details, they knew Kayla and Bethany were at war. Peers who might have been drawn in to a Christian community had no interest in joining the trip.

The point isn't that Christians can't disagree. But the girls turned their disagreement into a division that fractured the group and made their faith in Christ look fake.

Genuine unity has the opposite effect. It lets the world know that Jesus is real—and that the message of his love is really true. When we seek peace, others see Jesus.

I (Ken) remember the first time I saw this fact in action. I was friends with a young woman who was searching for spiritual meaning and feeling badly disillusioned with church. I invited her to worship one Sunday, thinking I might be able to change her mind.

Moments after we sat down, my pastor asked one of the church leaders to come forward. Suddenly I remembered that the two had argued heatedly—publicly—just the week before. I was already embarrassed. I assumed my pastor was about to reprimand this man in front of the whole church.

The pastor started by listing his own failings. He admitted to saying things that should have stayed private. He told us that he and the other man had later met to sort out their differences. Then he apologized for being a poor example.

I wanted to climb under my chair. My friend already had plenty of bad thoughts about church, and we were handing her more. I was so worried about what my friend was thinking that I barely noticed when the other man also owned up to his part of the fight.

On the drive home my friend said she couldn't believe what my pastor had done that morning. I held my breath, expecting a cynical slam on the church. That wasn't what came out of her mouth. Instead she said, "I've never seen a pastor do something like that. Could I come back next week?"

From then on, God had my friend's intense attention. Not much later, she became a Christian.

The Enemy of Peace

If peace is so crucial to our making a mark in the world, you can be sure that there's someone doing all he can to promote conflicts among believers. Satan, whose name means "adversary," likes nothing better than to see us at odds with one another.

Satan's lies are everywhere, in all the voices that tempt us to selfishness, greed, controversy, and dishonesty. He eggs us on with slogans like "Look out for number one," "I deserve better than this," "God doesn't expect me to stick around in an unhappy situation," "I'll forgive you, but I won't forget," and "Don't get mad, get even."

Though we hear Satan's messages every day, he himself is stealthy, flying low so we don't spot his role in our conflicts. As long as we think people are our only adversaries, we won't recognize him as our most dangerous enemy. That's unwise. God tells us to actively resist the schemes of Satan and his evil underlings, because "our struggle is not against flesh and blood, but against the rulers, against the authorities, against the powers of this dark world and against the spiritual forces of evil in the heavenly realms" (Eph. 6:12).

Strive like a Gladiator

Of course, we can't blame all conflict on Satan. We need to own our sins and help others do likewise. But in every conflict, we need to realize that all of us—no matter what side we are on—battle a mutual enemy who wants to destroy us. He is like a "roaring lion looking for someone to devour" (1 Peter 5:8).

Because our struggle for peace is a battle for our very lives, we should strive for peace with all our might. As Paul wrote, "Live a life worthy of the calling you have received. Be completely humble and gentle; be patient, bearing with one another in love. Make every effort to keep the unity of the Spirit through the bond of peace" (Eph. 4:1–3). The Greek word translated "make every effort"—*spoudazontes*—means to strive eagerly, earnestly, diligently. It's a word that a trainer of gladiators might have used when he sent men to fight to the death in the Colosseum: "*Spoudazontes!*" "Make every effort to stay alive today!"

Peace is worth that life-or-death effort. If you want to grab hold of all the peace God has for you, you have to give it your all.

Trust God, Do Good

The Lord's love surrounds those who trust him.

Psalm 32:10 NCV

Stranded on a snowy logging road in the coastal mountains of Oregon, James and Kati Kim and their two small daughters hunkered down in their Saab station wagon. For a couple days they kept warm by running the engine. When the gas ran dry, they burned anything that would catch fire—wood, magazines, even their car tires. Nine days later, desperate to save his family, James Kim struck out into a treacherous wilderness wearing only light clothes, a jacket, and tennis shoes, headed for a town he believed to be four miles away.

Two days after Kim left the car, rescuers located his wife and daughters. Somewhere around that time, Kim collapsed into a stream, hypothermic and exhausted. Those who found his body and retraced his route discovered he had traveled more than ten miles on foot, a feat they could only call "superhuman." Kim had circled back around almost to within sight of his family's car, though he remained cut off by a sheer cliff. Tragically, their car had been stranded only about a mile from Black Bear Lodge, a hunting resort with ample supplies for the winter.

After days of waiting to be rescued with no help in sight, the only thing that James Kim wanted was to find the way to safety for himself and his family. In the confusion of those excruciating hours on the mountain, he chose the wrong way home.

A Tough Road

In his Word, God marks out a clear path to peace, a process you are learning throughout this book. But in almost any conflict it can be far easier to find other ways to go. You see solutions that look quicker . . . easier . . . cheaper . . . more popular . . . more obvious. Yet what looks to our human eyes to be the right path can in God's view be wildly misguided.

When you choose to be a peacemaker, you will find that God leads you down paths that can be challenging. His way of handling conflict doesn't always make sense to people who don't know him. His expectations can even feel completely opposite of our own. When you face conflict, you might want to

- *Walk away from people who hurt you.* God says to stay engaged.
- *Bury all your feelings.* God wants you to speak up to him and others.
- *Jump on the small faults of others.* God teaches you to overlook petty offenses.
- *Do unto others before they do unto you.* God directs you to treat others the way you want to be treated.
- *Create a wall of toughness that shuts people out.* God asks you to be warm and welcoming.
- *Strike back at your enemies.* God says to love even people who hate you.

- *Talk down to people who oppose you.* God commands you to speak kindly to everyone.

When you sense God nudging you to walk down the path he maps out, you might wonder what he has in store for you. As you study the lay of the land, you might feel like you know the best way out of the situation and God has no clue what is going on. When you have to work intensely to slog through disagreements, you might question if your all-powerful, all-loving God is actually on your side.

Ready for the Journey

Your ability to do right, love others, and follow God's way of peace all come down to one thing: you have to know that God is worth trusting.

God isn't looking for blind obedience. The more you understand his love and power, the easier it is to trust him. The more you trust him, the easier it is to do his will. This is especially true when you are involved in conflict. If you believe God watches out for you with absolute power and total love, you will have what it takes to serve him as a peacemaker in even the roughest circumstances. If you don't trust him, you won't follow his path.

The Bible is full of stories about people who decided that God deserves this kind of trust. They were go-anywhere, do-anything, follow-no-matter-what kind of people because they understood the God they serve.

Take the apostle Paul, for example. He refused to fret about imprisonments, beatings, and his impending execution. The world was kicking his tail, yet he could say, "I am not ashamed, because I know whom I have believed, and am convinced that he is able to guard what I have entrusted to him for that day" (2 Tim. 1:12). God was watching over every part of Paul's life, including the state of his soul.

Jesus takes faith to another level, showing better than anyone what this trust looks like. When faced with the brutal suffering of the cross and an awful separation from his Father as he died to pay the penalty for our sins, Jesus felt a dread we can barely begin to comprehend. Yet he responded to his human fears with trust, accepting that God was in control of his situation: "My Father, if it is not possible for this cup to be taken away unless I drink it, may your will be done" (Matt. 26:42). Even at the moment he died, Jesus believed in God's care: "Father, into your hands I commit my spirit" (Luke 23:46).

Your Trustworthy God

God's *control*. God's *care*. Those are the prime qualities that make God worth trusting.

Suppose you found yourself living in the most dangerous neighborhood of a sprawling city. Gunshots frequently ring through the air. Thieves lurk in the darkness to break into your home. You never feel completely certain whether the people you meet on the street are friend or foe.

Left on your own, you would do everything you could to crawl out of town in a hurry. But suppose you had a protector. Someone awesomely powerful. Someone who cared for you with unquestionable loyalty. You might dare to stay.

In your perilous world, God is that kind of protector. You have surely noticed that bad things happen in life. Situations get almost too complex to work out. Acting as a peacemaker can at times cause you pain. But you can endure if you are convinced beyond any doubt that God has your back.

God Is Total Power

Jesus and Paul trusted the Father because they had their facts straight. They knew their Lord was aware of everything that impacted their lives. Not only that, he was in complete control of everything that happened to them. This "sovereignty of God" is a deep topic. But it's a truth that helps you be a peacemaker.

To be "sovereign" means to rule supreme over every other power, exercising ultimate control over all things. Only God possesses that all-powerful strength. His reign reaches over all creation and every human organization and government. He alone controls the lives and destinies of individual human beings. He watches over events as small as a sparrow's fall from a tree (see Matt. 10:29).

God isn't like a mighty CEO of a multinational corporation exercising colossal power from a distance or relating to the human race as a mass of anonymous people. God takes a deep personal interest in every individual to such a degree that he knows the smallest details of our lives. That kind of loving attention baffles our minds. When King David tried to grasp the wonders of God's intimate involvement in his life, he was stunned. "Such knowledge is too wonderful for me," he said, "too lofty for me to attain" (Ps. 139:6). No other being in the universe knows you fully and still loves you totally.

Here's a point that's truly crucial for peacemaking: God's sovereignty is so complete that he exercises ultimate control even over painful and unjust events. He not only knows when he points us down a difficult path. He is sovereign over every tough thing we encounter.

Be straight about this: God hates evil. He never sins. Yet he sometimes allows suffering and permits people to do evil, even though he has the power to stop them.

Nowhere is this more obvious than when the apostle Peter confronted the people who had tried and executed Jesus: "This man was handed over to you *by God's set purpose and foreknowledge*; and you, with the help of wicked men, put him to death by nailing him to the cross" (Acts 2:23, emphasis added). Jesus didn't die because God had lost control or was

41

looking the other direction. God was fully in control at all times. He chose to let evil people kill his Son so Jesus could save the world.

Not only did God's control extend to the life and death of his Son, but his reach also extends to everything going on in your family, your friends, your school, your job, your every waking and dozing moment. Even when sinful and painful things are happening, God is somehow exercising ultimate control and working things out for his good purposes. As tough as it is to hear, trials mature you. They are often times when God grabs our attention to draw us to himself.

Nothing in life happens by chance. We will never suffer trials or get caught in a dispute unless God allows it. We can be sure that because God is all-powerful, he has his eye on every conflict that comes into our lives. Knowing that he personally looks out for us at every moment is one reason we can walk through conflict with confidence. But it's only part of the story.

God Is Totally Good

The fact that God allows tough things to happen in our lives can be really mind-bending for us to hear, because we often measure God's actions by our own ideas of right and wrong. Something inside us says, "If I were God and could control everything in the world, I wouldn't allow someone to suffer like that." We are especially quick to judge God if the *someone* who is suffering is *us*.

We get past that difficulty only when we get a full picture of God. It's true: if total power were God's only trait, we would have loads of reasons to fear. We would expect him to wield his power randomly, like the villain in a bad sci-fi movie wildly aiming a planet-melting laser here and there.

That isn't the God we meet in Scripture. Not only is the Lord all-powerful, he is all-loving. Psalm 62:11–12 shouts his perfection: "You, O God, are strong, and . . . you, O Lord, are loving." We trust God because we count on both his control and his care. Our lives are wrapped not just in his power but also in his love. As Psalm 32:10 says, "The Lord's love surrounds those who trust him" (NCV).

It's one thing to accept these facts about God intellectually. It's another to let them rule the way we see life.

I (Kevin) was stuck in the worst conflict of my life. Months into a new position working with at-risk teens, I felt sure God had abandoned me. I constantly clashed with my boss. I felt powerless to stop what I saw as fatal blunders within the organization. Worse yet, my best efforts to escape to a new job failed. As time stretched on, my frustration turned to a burning pain.

I had a friend who was newly married, happy in his ministry, humming along like his whole life was sweet. In a conversation with me he summed up his mood with a line from the old film *Chariots of Fire*, a movie where the main character competes all the way to the 1924 Olympics. As he competed, this real-life runner, Eric Liddell, sensed he was doing exactly what God wanted him to do. He said, "When I run, I feel his pleasure."

At the time I heard those words from my friend and said to myself, "I don't feel God's pleasure. Right now I think I feel God's anger." I didn't sense that he was anywhere near me. I struggled to see his power and his care.

My mind knew God cared for me. But my heart felt like God's love and power should solve everything. My feelings, however, didn't reflect the facts of the situation. God saw what was going on at work. Through it all, he watched over me, my family, and my co-workers. In time he led me to a better spot. Even if he hadn't, he was still in charge. He was with me whatever I went through, because he is not only totally powerful but also completely kind.

God-Trusters in the Bible

The Bible is filled with stories of people who experienced all kinds of mishaps, yet worked through their misgivings to trust in God. You know about people like David, Peter, and Paul, but consider these:

- **Job:** This man's whole prosperous life was blown away, and he loudly voiced many doubts. Even so, he eventually said to God, "I know that you can do all things; no plan of yours can be thwarted" (Job 42:2). And he admitted he couldn't begin to grasp God's good purposes.
- **Joseph:** The favorite son of an elderly father, Joseph was so despised by his older brothers that they sold him into slavery. In spite of his struggles he served God faithfully, even when he was unjustly imprisoned. In time Joseph attained great power and forgave the brothers who had hurt him. He said, "You intended to harm me, but God intended it for good" (Gen. 50:20).
- **Deborah:** This Old Testament woman was appalled that a man wouldn't lead Israel's forces into battle. Rather than allow her nation to be crushed, she accompanied the commander into battle, exercising courageous faith when few people trusted God. She sang a song of victory in Judges 5.
- **Esther:** A woman chosen as queen of Persia in an ancient beauty pageant, Esther hid her Jewish roots even as her people were threatened with extermination. But she was no empty-headed toy for the king; she overcame fear to walk her God-appointed path as deliverer of her people. She heeded the Lord's words to her through her uncle Mordecai, who said, "Who knows, you may have been chosen queen for just such a time as this" (Esther 4:4 NCV).

You might be thinking, "That was then. This is now. The giants of the Bible might have been able to trust God during conflict, but they don't live in my world." But courageous people still step out in trust, making bold choices to go where God points them.

Trust Is Your Choice

Trusting God doesn't mean we never have questions, doubts, or fears. We can't shut down our normal human reactions to harsh circumstances. But trusting God means that *in spite of our questions, doubts, and fears*, we continue to count on two facts: God is always in control, and God always cares.

Warren and Donna Pett were Wisconsin dairy farmers when they started volunteering in the junior high ministry that I (Kevin) led. They were as real as people get—good, godly folk. Year after year Donna led a group of seventh-grade girls, and she helped me lead several camps and trips. Warren was a strong bear of a man who helped lead our sixth-grade boys. I had all three of their children—Marita, Saul, and Ezra—in my youth group.

The Petts were still in their forties when they sold their family farm and headed to Africa as missionaries. After a stint doing youth ministry and providing support services in Kenya, they moved to Uganda, where Warren taught agriculture and Bible courses at a Christian college while Donna taught cooking and tailoring.

One evening in March 2004, Warren and Donna returned to their thatched hut after leading devotions for students, teachers, and staff. Shortly thereafter, seven armed men came searching for money at the school. While two poured gasoline on a missionary vehicle and grass homes and lit them on fire, five others approached the Petts' home. The men called for Warren and Donna to come out and then opened fire, killing them and a student who tried to warn them.

Whenever we follow God's path as peacemakers, we step into danger. That doesn't mean we will be killed for our faith, but bringing the peace of Jesus to the world does put us in the line of fire. The strife we face shapes us to be more like Jesus, and it allows people to see who our Lord really is.

Whatever we encounter, we can count on God's control and care. When he leads us into a situation, he always knows what awaits us and how he will carry us through. As Warren Pett wrote in a letter before leaving for Africa, "Donna and I do not necessarily know the road ahead, but we take comfort in knowing the One who made and is in control of the road."

The question is this: do you trust God enough to follow him wherever he leads you, even if the path looks difficult—even impossible? You can only go forward when you realize that your all-powerful, all-loving God is truly on your side. If you want to be one of God's go-anywhere, do-anything, follow-no-matter-what kind of people, trust is what keeps you walking down God's path.

G2.
GET THE LOG OUT OF YOUR EYE

First take the plank out of your own eye, and then you will see clearly to remove the speck from your brother's eye.

Matthew 7:5

Olivia's little brother was a mess, no doubt about it. Almost six years younger than his big sister, Zach could wipe out a room in minutes, splattering from corner to corner assorted action figures, remote-control vehicles, and sports equipment.

Olivia was mad that the family room was almost always littered with Zach's stuff. She was tense and embarrassed about anyone coming over without lots of warning. But one day when Olivia hollered at Zach to pick up after himself, he just lifted a finger and pointed straight at his big sister's bedroom.

If the family room sometimes looked like a trash can had been turned upside down, then Olivia's room often seemed more like a garbage truck had backed up to the window and dumped its contents. The floor was covered with outfits she had tried on and decided not to wear. There were stacks of homework assignments half completed—and heaps of papers graded and handed back long ago. All of Olivia's things were literally piled up.

Olivia had always reasoned that the clutter in her bedroom was *her* mess in *her* room—and she could just shut the door. It dawned on Olivia, though, that the state of her room annoyed the rest of her family at least as much as Zach's untidiness did. And her own mess was often the biggest reason she couldn't invite friends over to the house.

That weekend Olivia straightened up her room top to bottom. She made a list to stick on her mirror—five ways she was going to do better at keeping the house picked up. Four had to do with keeping her own things straightened up. The fifth was her plan to help teach Zach how to pick up after himself.

We are all quick to slam others for their faults when we ourselves have bigger failings. It's what Jesus talked about in Matthew 7:3–5:

> Why do you look at the speck of sawdust in your brother's eye and pay no attention to the plank in your own eye? How can you say to your brother, "Let me take the speck out of your eye," when all the time there is a plank in your own eye? You hypocrite, first take the plank out of your own eye, and then you will see clearly to remove the speck from your brother's eye.

That passage contains one of the most vivid images in the entire Bible. Jesus pictures a person with a log jutting from his eye—yet that same person is trying to delicately dab a speck of dust out of someone else's eye. Blinded by his own big problem, the first guy is a hypocrite for trying to help another. He first needs to take care of his own fault.

Jesus doesn't mean that our own sins are necessarily bigger or worse than those of others. But they are obvious. Right under our noses. Completely under our control. And they should be the first thing we examine and correct when conflict hits.

You might read Jesus's words and jump to the conclusion that you should never get face-to-face with people to point out their failings. But if you read that passage carefully, you'll realize it doesn't tell you to always keep mum about others' flaws. Instead, it warns us against correcting others too quickly or aiming our criticism in the wrong direction. Before we talk to others about their faults, we need to make sure we have owned up to ours. Once we take care of the plank in our own eye, then we are in good shape to get the speck out of someone else's. If we have dealt with *our* contribution to a conflict, we can legitimately approach others about *theirs*.

As we try to see our own part of a problem, we often find we have two kinds of faults. One has to do with our inner thoughts and feelings, the other with our outward actions. First, we might have an *overly sensitive attitude*. Don't get us wrong. Sensitivity is an awesome quality in both guys and girls. But here we are talking about being offended too easily by how people treat us. We need to get over that. Second, we may have contributed to the conflict through our own *sinful behavior*. What we have done or not done in a situation might have made a clash worse. We also need to learn to clean up those messes.

Solving an issue between us and someone else means addressing both kinds of problems. So in the next chapter we will look hard at our own attitude issues. In the following two chapters we will see how to put a stop to actions that jeopardize peace.

When we are stuck in a conflict, the last place we want to look—at our own faults—is actually the first place to start. "G2" stands for "Get the log out."

Get Over It

A man's wisdom gives him patience; it is to his glory
to overlook an offense.

Proverbs 19:11

You can almost always count on a behind-the-wheel driving
test to be a tense, sweaty experience. Having accumulated
hours of book learning and far more hours practicing on real-
life roads, you head to a test station. A clipboard-wielding
examiner climbs into your car and, without a single hopeful
word, points you to a course designed to verify your skills
and expose your incompetence.

So you sit up straight. You grip the wheel with both
hands. When you come to a stop, you pause for emphasis.
As you study the intersection, you look left . . . then right
. . . then left again, not merely flicking a glance from side
to side but turning your whole head to scan for traffic. Out
of the corner of your eye you spot the examiner scoring

your moves. You cringe. At the end of the test—assuming you haven't ended early for committing illegalities or colliding with something—you listen humbly as the examiner recounts your every mistake and reveals your score.

Under the Microscope

Imagine living your whole life under that kind of careful inspection! You can be sure that your parents, their insurance company, the local police, and everyone who lives on your block rejoice that your skills are systematically scrutinized before you obtain a license to steer a ton or two of steel around your neighborhood . . . but not everything in life is as deadly serious as good driving. Most of what happens isn't nearly that big of a deal. And none of us wants to live in a world where people with clipboards and pens critique our every move. We wouldn't be thrilled if at the end of each day we were presented with a minute-by-minute report on our every thought, word, and action—especially a report that found some kind of fault with everything we did.

As much as we dislike that thought, we can be quick to aim intense scrutiny at others. Even though we want others to go easy on us, we might feel eager to judge others harshly. That is especially true when we directly clash with others. Even though we expect others to excuse our faults, we often pounce on others when they wrong us.

Peacemaking is a radical choice to pursue God's way of dealing with every clash you face. But you might assume that your commitment to act as a peacemaker means you should immediately wade into a situation to work it out. If a teacher reprimands you unfairly, you should instantaneously confront her on the mix-up. When a friend says something hurtful, you should straighten out your insensitive friend. Or if a teammate misses a play, you should take it upon yourself to explain the advantages of bump-set-spike over going for a kill from the back row.

Actually, those choices aren't always the best path to peacemaking. There is a first step to consider. Instead of jumping in to address the wrongdoing, *you can choose to let it go.*

Looking Past Offenses

Those men and women who evaluate driving skills might seem to strive to catch every picky fault. Yet they don't. As particular as they first appear, they don't knock off points just because your death grip on the wheel makes your knuckles turn white. They don't scold you for veering from the center of a lane by an inch or two. And they won't fail you for making a clumsy right turn. Driver's license examiners actually look for relatively major deficiencies in how you handle a vehicle. As they guide you through real streets or an artificial course, they get a sense of whether you will drive safely. In the process they do an amazing thing. They overlook some of your little faults.

In many situations of life, the best way to resolve a conflict is simply to overlook the wrongs others do to you.

We don't often observe people dropping the matter . . . covering over . . . being patient . . . putting up with . . . forgiving. Almost everywhere we look—school, friends, teams, home, even church—the ability to overlook a fault is rare. Yet it's how God treats us. He lavishes us with astonishing goodness and forgiveness. Check what Psalm 103:8–10 says about his attitude toward us: "The LORD is compassionate and gracious, slow to anger, abounding in love. He will not always accuse, nor will he harbor his anger forever; he does not treat us as our sins deserve or repay us according to our iniquities." God doesn't deal harshly with us when we sin. And God's deep love for us shows us a fresh way to approach others.

What the Bible Says about Overlooking

Overlooking comes highly recommended throughout Scripture. Start with this blunt insight from the Bible's book of wisdom, Proverbs:

A man's wisdom gives him patience; it is to his glory to overlook an offense.
Proverbs 19:11

There is more:

Starting a quarrel is like breaching a dam; so drop the matter before a dispute breaks out.
Proverbs 17:14

Above all, love each other deeply, because love covers over a multitude of sins.
1 Peter 4:8

Be completely humble and gentle; be patient, bearing with one another in love.
Ephesians 4:2

Bear with each other and forgive whatever grievances you may have against one another. Forgive as the Lord forgave you.
Colossians 3:13

A New View

Every morning before school Julia paced the living room, veering from her path only to turn to look again and again out the front window. With her jacket on and her book bag shouldered, she sometimes stomped a foot in anger, wondering why Cody was late yet again. With each passing minute, she had less time at school before the first bell rang.

Her neighbor was great about giving her rides to and from school, and the only cost was an occasional gas card. But Julia fumed when Cody came late. Most days their arrival at school cut too close for her comfort.

Julia's mom saw her frustration and suggested she try to see the situation from Cody's point of view. He was an upper-classman and didn't want to spend any more time at school than he had to. While Julia missed some social time before school with her freshman friends, she and Cody never once arrived so late that she couldn't get to her locker and make it to homeroom on time. And Cody was a more trustworthy chauffeur than anyone else she knew.

Julia decided that the situation called more for gratitude than anger. She chose to overlook what was really a small annoyance and focus on taking care of her own part of the issue. She decided to be ready at the same time each morning, in case Cody came early. And instead of packing up her bag and pacing the floor, she grabbed a book, sat back in a chair with a clear view of the driveway, and enjoyed a few minutes of reading before he showed up.

Overlooking Isn't a Cop-Out

Overlooking is an *active* choice. It isn't a fake peace where you chicken out of confrontation, staying silent for the moment but filing away the offense to use against someone later. That's actually a form of denial, and you can be sure it leads to a bitterness that eventually explodes in anger. When you overlook another person's faults, you deliberately decide not to brood over an offense. You stop replaying the situation in your mind. You quit talking about it. You choose to let it go.

Overlooking is a *strong* choice. It isn't a broken peace where you go through life battle-ready, on high alert, locked and loaded like a rifle prepared for firing at anyone who crosses you. Overlooking is powered by all the strength of the gospel. Some people argue against overlooking by saying, "It isn't right to let people off easy." I (Ken) have a quick answer to that. Whenever I hear a Christian speak those words, I ask, "Where would you spend eternity if God dealt us justice with no mercy?" The answer is obvious: we would all be condemned to hell. Fortunately, God doesn't treat us as our sins deserve. To those who have trusted in Christ, he is compassionate and merciful—and he expects us to treat one another the same way. As Jesus taught, "Be merciful, just as your Father is merciful" (Luke 6:36).

Overlooking is a *practical* choice. It isn't an exasperating peace where you constantly correct others in the name of peace. That kind of "peace" would cause our world to screech to a halt. Each of us has abundant shortcomings, and calling each other to account for every fault could occupy us from now until eternity. By overlooking smaller offenses, we create an atmosphere of grace where we can let go of hurt and move on with life.

When You Should—and Shouldn't—Let It Go

Overlooking is a peacemaker's first option in responding to conflict. In fact, it's the choice to consider before you even begin to think of taking other steps to correct a situation. But overlooking isn't the only option. Sometimes it isn't the right option. Overlooking clearly isn't the way to go when a wrong

- creates a wall between you and the other person
- makes you feel differently toward someone for an extended time

- causes serious hurt to the offender
- inflicts significant harm on the victim
- does obvious damage to God's reputation

Sometimes you know right away that a single wrong action is far too big to overlook. Other times a fault goes on and on, becoming a pattern in another person's life. While the offense might not be huge, the abrasive effect grinds at your relationship. As time passes, you realize that you can't let the problem go any longer. You need to go to that person and get the problem straightened out, using the specific strategies you will pick up later in this book. And sometimes you just need to ask God for wisdom to know what to do.

You can again think about your options in terms of real-life habits on the road. Even safe drivers make stupid mistakes. Like they don't signal in time. They misjudge a situation and pull out in front of you just a tad too close. Or you pop into their blind spot and they accidentally cut you off. Actually, they make all the same mistakes you make from time to time. Overlooking means treating others the way we want to be treated, giving them the same grace-filled tolerance we wish others would give us.

Those minor faults, however, are clearly different from driving on the wrong side of the yellow line or crashing a car into a sidewalk café and maiming people as they lunch. The right response to those offenses is the blare of a horn or a squad car ride to do time behind bars. Overlooking works for minor hurts—the small bumps of everyday life. It isn't the right strategy for handling more major wrongs.

Check Your Attitude—and Change It

Even if you are convinced that overlooking seems like the smart choice for many situations, that doesn't mean overlooking comes easily. For all our feelings that overlooking seems like the right thing to do, other feelings rise up to tell us to hang on to our hurt.

There is hardly a human alive who doesn't have difficulty letting go of wrongs done to us. We scribble about them in notebooks and diaries. We retell them to our friends, who most often reinforce our views of just how right we are. We talk to ourselves, looping audio tracks of harsh things we have heard said to our faces or behind our backs. Our minds might even play back full-color videos of wrongs we have suffered.

One reason we can find it tough to overlook offenses is that we have an overly sensitive attitude—a tendency to dwell on what others have done to us. God is so aware of this inclination that he gave us some specific instructions in his Word on how to deal with it. He wants us to guard against this problem by checking our attitudes.

Paul's letter to the Philippians shows how to examine our attitudes during a conflict. Apparently Paul had heard that two followers of Jesus in Philippi were quarrelling. As part of his open letter to the church in that city, Paul took time to poke at these two female friends to seek peace: "I plead with Euodia and I plead with Syntyche to agree with each other in the Lord" (Phil. 4:2).

Can you imagine having your name etched in the pages of the Bible for people to know henceforth and forevermore about your conflict? Paul doesn't divulge what the argument was about, but maybe everyone already knew. He doesn't tell which woman was in the wrong, yet he says that if each would rearrange her thinking "in the Lord," their disharmony would vanish. Paul doesn't even lay out exactly what these women should do, but surely some words he penned earlier in his letter apply to their situation: "Do nothing out of selfish ambition or vain conceit, but in humility consider others better than yourselves. Each of you should look not only to your own interests, but also to the interests of others" (Phil. 2:3–4).

For Paul, it's all about attitude. He instructs these women and the rest of the church to quit thinking so much about themselves and instead consider the interests of others—their needs, desires, and dreams. He invites them to give up their rights.

What about "My Rights"?

Overlooking might feel like a setup to always be the one who gets the short end of a deal, the one who always endures unjust treatment, the stereotypical Christian doormat who always lies down so others can stomp on your back and wipe mud on your shirt. Overlooking might feel like others have all the rights in the world and you have none.

If you think that overlooking means surrendering some rights, you are getting a clear view of the situation. When you overlook, you give up the right to hold on to your hurt. You give up the right to speak freely about the subject. You give up the right to expect punishment for the person who offended you. You give up the right to moral superiority. Honestly, you give up the right to be right.

Surrendering even the tiniest of rights offends our deep sense of fairness. But the Bible teaches that it's better to be wronged than to wrongly assert our rights. "Why not rather be wronged?" Paul asks (1 Cor. 6:7). Exercising our rights can trigger more harm than good—causing a conflict to live on rather than putting it to rest. We have legal rights that don't match up to how God wants us to live: "pleading the fifth" and refusing to testify about our own wrongdoing, for example, rather than owning up to our sin. Pressing for our rights can make us pushy, creating a scene where we come off as incredibly selfish rather than amazingly caring.

The Bible does say it can be appropriate to exercise our rights by talking with others about their wrongs and holding them totally accountable. After Paul was beaten in Philippi, for example, he insisted that the government authorities apologize for their unjust conduct (see Acts 16:35–39).

But on a day-to-day, person-to-person level, surrendering our rights is often the path that leads to peace. It's the example we see in Jesus, who willingly laid down his right to justice by allowing himself to be crucified as a substitute for our sin (see 1 Peter 2:22–25). It's a chance to show mercy to people who don't deserve it, just like God showed mercy to us. And to be absolutely practical, surrendering our rights can be the quickest way to end a conflict that isn't worth dragging on.

Is This Worth a Fight?

Earlier this school year I (Kevin) watched my son, Nate, face a situation that put this point to the test. One day he received a detention notice from the dean's office at his high school. One of his teachers had reported Nate absent, an offense that carries an automatic penalty of an hour in the school slammer.

Nate is known for his crazy humor, not for cutting class. When he approached the teacher who reported him absent, he discovered that his alleged nonappearance occurred several weeks back in time. Christmas break had come and gone, and the teacher's memory of the day was long gone. He just knew what his grade book said. My wife and I also knew that if Nate had skipped even a single class, we would have received a computer-generated phone call the same day. There had been no call. Despite the dubious evidence, the teacher wouldn't back down.

Nate faced a choice. I suggested he go sit for an hour after school. In almost thirteen years of school he had never served detention. I joked that it would be educational. A good story. But between his homework, job, and after-school activities, Nate didn't have an hour to waste. He also hated the idea that his teacher thought he was being dishonest.

What he faced was a choice to surrender his rights. To overlook a wrong. To just get over it and move on. Or to do something to resolve the situation. Nate had to decide whether pressing the issue was worth it. As he weighed his options, the incident was bumped up to the vice principal. When she summoned Nate to her office, he grabbed the chance to make his case. He persuaded her that he had done nothing to deserve detention, so the matter was resolved without a fight.

If we are straight-up objective about the issues we face in life, most of our conflicts simply aren't worth a fight. We focus on what we think is the high price of overlooking. We should also count the enormous cost of *not* overlooking.

In every conflict we have to ask ourselves, "Is this really worth fighting over?" When the issues are big, the answer is yes. But when the issues are small, the answer should be no. Our determination to hang on to an issue can hand us a huge bill in wasted time, energy, and money—costs that are easy to miss when we are caught up in what seems like an all-important clash.

At first glance, "letting it go" or "getting over it" looks like an awful way out of conflict. But as a peacemaker, overlooking isn't just your first option. Often it's your fastest and least costly route to peace, and it's one of God's best ideas.

The State of Your Heart

What causes fights and quarrels among you? Don't
they come from your desires that battle within you?

James 4:1

I (Ken) am a normal dad. When I come home from a long
day at the office, I would like to unwind in an oasis of do-
mestic peace and tranquility. Because I am a normal dad in
a normal family, however, that doesn't always happen.

I remember a time when my kids, Megan and Jeff, had
been at each other all week. Their squabbling had exhausted
the patience of their usually calm mom. Corlette found herself resorting to sharp words, complete with threats of "Wait
until your father comes home!" Instead of walking through
the door and finding smiling children and a serene, affec-
tionate wife, I discovered grim faces and harsh voices. Home
felt like a war zone.

Corlette and I worked to break the cycle of conflict, but it
always restarted within hours. By Sunday I felt frustrated and

even resentful toward my children. That morning Corlette went to church early for a meeting. I would follow thirty minutes later with the kids. As we approached the car, a new battle erupted.

"It's my turn to sit in the front seat!"

"No, you got to yesterday!"

"Well, you shouldn't sit there anyway. You're so small the airbag could kill you."

"I don't care! I'm not sitting in the backseat."

A new voice broke into the exchange. Mine. I shouted, "Be quiet!" Pointing to my daughter and son in turn, I told them each exactly what they would do. "You get in the backseat right now—you, front seat. I don't want to hear another word out of either of you!"

As I climbed into the car, I adjusted the rearview mirror so I could glare at Megan as I lectured her in the backseat. Venting the anger that had been building in me all week, I promised my kids I would make things miserable for them. I told them how angry I was at the way they had been acting. When I finally paused for air, Jeffrey saw his opening.

"Daddy," he said meekly, "do you think you should pray to Jesus and ask him if it's rightful anger?"

Jeff's words cut me to the core. I saw an empty parking lot and pulled in. Before I had even shut off the car, I knew what I needed to say. Turning to my kids, I went to the heart of our conflict. My behavior that morning is summed up with painful accuracy in James 4:1–3:

> What causes fights and quarrels among you? Don't they come from your desires that battle within you? You want something but don't get it. You kill and covet, but you cannot have what you want. You quarrel and fight. You do not have, because you do not ask God. When you ask, you do not receive, because you ask with wrong motives, that you may spend what you get on your pleasures.

Unmet desires in our hearts are the most basic cause of conflict. When we want something and think that we won't be satisfied until we get it, that desire begins to eat at us. And control us. If others fail to fulfill our desires, we go to war with them. If our wants continue to go unmet, we fight even harder to get our way. It's a hurtful, violent, even deadly progression. Let's look at how it all goes down one step at a time.

Working Out Your Wants

Conflict always starts with some kind of desire. Some wants are always wrong, like revenge, lust, or greed. But many desires are good as long as we pursue them in the right time, right way, and right amount. Nothing is inherently wrong with wanting peace and quiet. It's normal to want close relationships and to be accepted by our peers. Or to want to make good grades. Or to live in a decent house, go to an interesting job, and enjoy new clothes or electronics. It's great to find success in life and earn enough money to cover hobbies, travel, or adventures that recharge us. These are all good gifts from God, and it's more than okay when we seek them within the boundaries of God's commands.

But what if someone stands in the way of a good desire? You still don't have to give up on fulfilling your wish. You can talk to that person, whether it's a parent, sister, brother, friend, peer, boss, or even someone you see as an enemy. You can work to discover ways you can benefit each other. You can invite outside assistance to help you find a win-win solution.

But what if another person constantly fails to satisfy you? If he happens to be your boss, you might need to hunt for a new job. But it's far less okay to walk away from a longtime friend or fellow believer. And you don't have that option at all if the other person is your parent—or your spouse or child. Unmet desires never justify cutting off those relationships.

Whenever you find yourself in a situation where it looks like your desires will never be met, you face a choice between two courses of action.

Tough but rewarding, the first route starts with trusting God and seeking your fulfillment in him and him alone. The Old Testament songwriter Asaph voiced this uncommon attitude: "Whom have I in heaven but you? And earth has nothing I desire besides you" (Ps. 73:25). When God is your grandest desire in life, you can be content with his plans for you. You can ask him to keep you growing and maturing no matter what the other person does. And you can continue to pray for people who block your desire, asking for God's best for them and waiting for the Lord to alter your situation if and when he chooses.

This first course is a radical decision to desire God above anything else, letting God reign in your life as he so fully deserves. It's a decision God promises to bless. He vows to use your difficult situation to make you like his Son. As you trust him, you can gain astonishing encouragement from his promise to work for your good in even the worst situations of life: "And we know that in all things God works for the good of those who love him, who have been called according to his purpose. For those God foreknew he also predestined to be conformed to the likeness of his Son" (Rom. 8:28–29).

Going Your Own Way

With God's help, trusting him is a wonderfully peace-filled way to do life. But when we feel stuck in a situation full of disappointed desires, it's exceedingly easy to choose a different course. We keep fighting to get what we long for, driven by desire and dissatisfaction. At the least, we wallow in self-pity, letting our hearts be overwhelmed with bitterness toward people who block our way. At the worst, we push ahead to grab what we want, destroying relationships and pulling away from God.

"I felt like I was right," Mya says as she remembers back to middle school. "At the time, I would have said I *knew* I was right." Mya had always thought her parents' expectations were overly strict—rules about where she could go, what she could do, and who she could hang out with. "I felt like my parents gave me no room to make my own choices. They hovered over me, so I had no space with my friends. They kept giving me speeches about not hanging out with 'those kinds of people,' but secretly that was my crowd. I didn't care what those friends were into. They liked me. So I would get out of the house whenever I could. I thought I was smart enough to make all of my own decisions. I wanted to feel independent."

On the surface Mya conformed to her parents' rules. Out of their sight she ran wild. Because she always checked in by phone and never missed curfew, her parents didn't catch on to her double life. Late in her freshman year Mya was caught drinking, and a drug test detected marijuana in her system. Her parents' trust in her was severely shaken. Mya is now substance-free, but she wishes she didn't have to take random drug tests to prove it. For a time, she has had less independence than ever.

Mya took a good thing—a normal desire to learn to make choices and be independent—and turned it absolutely wrong side up. By wanting a right thing in the wrong time, wrong way, and wrong amount, she made her unmet desire more important than her parents' rules and God's expectations. She made independence an idol.

The Birth of an Idol—*"I Desire"*

When we let our desires push God from his rightful first place in our lives, we have begun to worship another god.

Instead of letting the Lord reign as the King of our lives, we allow our wants to dominate us. Whatever it is we desire, we don't just wish for it a little bit. We want it *now*, we want it in *extreme quantities*, and we want it *however we can get it*. In fact, we want it *more than we want God*. That is idolatry.

You might think of idolatry as a pagan issue. If we check back to the Old Testament, though, we notice that idols were a massive problem, not just for the neighbors of Israel who lacked knowledge of the one true God, but also for the people of Israel themselves. They frequently tried to mix the worship of God with the worship of idols. As 2 Kings 17:41 describes, "Even while these people were worshiping the LORD, they were serving their idols." Whenever we exalt anything to a place higher than God, we are no different than the ancient Israelites.

You might picture an idol as a statue made of wood, stone, or metal—a man-made object standing in the temple of a fabricated deity. An idol is far broader and more personal than that. It is anything other than God that we rely on to be happy, fulfilled, or secure. In biblical terms, an idol is something other than God that

- captures our heart—our fascination, energy, and affection
- dominates our thoughts—our attention, fears, and sense of right and wrong
- controls our behavior—our time, money, words, and actions

In short, an idol is anything we love and pursue more than God. As Martin Luther wrote, "To whatever we look for any good thing and for refuge in every need, that is what is meant by 'god.' To have a god is nothing else than to trust and believe in him from the heart. . . . To whatever you give your heart and entrust your being, that, I say, is really your god."[1]

Even sincere Christians struggle with idolatry. We may believe in God and say we want to serve only him, but at times we allow other influences to rule us. We may still go to church, pray to God, and read the Bible, but an idol dictates our lives. That false god might be something inherently wrong. Or it can be a good desire gone bad, having grown so strong that it overpowers us.

Recognizing False Gods in Your Life—*"I Demand"*

So how do you know when a desire has become an idol in your life? It's when your heart moves from "I desire" to "I demand." You might notice it in how you think—you don't just wish for a thing, you regard it as a necessity to your happiness. Or you can hear it in a sometimes-subtle shift in your words—you don't just say you want something, you say you will die without it. Or you can spot it in your actions—you don't merely work hard to obtain something, you are willing to do wrong to get it. Your heart has moved from *great-to-have-it* to *got-to-have-it*.

A few years back my (Kevin's) doctor had questions about how my heart was functioning, so he referred me to a cardiologist. The heart doctor ordered an echocardiogram, a test in which a technician traced my chest with a wand that looks like a bar-code scanner. On a black-and-white monitor in the exam room, up popped an ultrasonic image of my heart—the same kind of picture doctors probably shot of you when you were safe in your mother's womb. The ultrasound revealed facts about my heart that were otherwise invisible, like its size, shape, position, and thickness.

Do you want to determine whether a good desire might be turning into a sinful demand? You can start by prayerfully asking yourself some penetrating questions that reveal the spiritual condition of your heart:

- What desire crowds other thoughts from my mind?
- How would I complete this sentence: "If only _____, then I would be happy, fulfilled, and secure"?
- What unmet desire makes me frustrated, anxious, resentful, bitter, angry, or depressed?
- What do I want so much that I am willing to hurt others to get it?

Just as I underwent tests to discover the truth about my physical heart, we all need to submit ourselves to this kind of spiritual heart check.

Criticizing and Condemning—"I Judge"

When an idol rules our hearts, our reasonable desires turn into unruly demands. When our demands consume us, we move further down the path of idolatry. We begin to judge other people. Think about it. When someone fails to satisfy us and falls short of our expectations, what is often the first thing we do? We criticize them. Or outright condemn them. Sometimes we keep our thoughts to ourselves, though often we blurt them out loud. More than thinking "I desire" or even "I demand," we move to "I judge."

It's tempting to imagine that our bitter thoughts or biting words don't matter much. Honestly, we all have negative thoughts toward others. We are surrounded by harsh words, even when their meanness is wrapped in humor and sarcasm.

We need to evaluate our judging, however, from God's point of view. Whenever we judge others, we attempt to take God's place. We assume we are qualified to fill God's shoes as Judge of the universe. Not only that, but in our grab for his power we imitate none other than the devil himself. God alone has the right to declare human beings guilty—or not guilty—so when we condemn others for not giving us what we want, we try to take God's place, just like the devil does. It's a setup for excruciating conflict.

Let's be clear on what judging is and isn't. Being able to discern when someone is sinning is an essential skill for every Christian. The Bible tells us to observe and weigh others' behavior so that we avoid joining in their sin and at times can correct them with loving concern. We become sinful judges, however, when we harbor feelings of superiority, condemnation, bitterness, or resentment. Judging often involves guessing at others' motives. It can mean we don't give people room to disagree with us or act differently from us. Most of all, judging reveals our lack of genuine love for others, because all we notice is their failure to meet our demands. When these attitudes are present, our judging is out of line. Sinful. We are playing God. People sense our condemnation of them, and conflict rages on.

Making Them Pay—*"I Punish"*

You can probably imagine a bad old movie in which a young damsel is thrown into the smoking mouth of a volcano to appease a jungle god. Maybe in social studies class you have read about actual human sacrifices practiced by ancient peoples. Or maybe you know something about Israel's Old Testament neighbors, who killed their children in hideous worship rituals to the pagan gods Baal and Molech.

One fact is clear: idols always demand sacrifices. When someone fails to satisfy our expectations, our idol says he should suffer. Whether deliberately or unconsciously, we find ways to hurt people so that they cave in to our desires. We might lash out with our tongues . . . shoot dirty looks . . . pout . . . start rumors . . . split friendships . . . give a cold shoulder . . . crush hopes and dreams . . . or resort to physical or sexual violence. Even if we don't use obviously sinful methods to punish others, we manage to find subtle ways to inflict pain. We stop only when people give us what we want.

When we catch ourselves punishing others in any way, we know that something other than God rules us. It's a sure sign that an idol owns our hearts.

God's Cure for an Idolatrous Heart

Only one cure exists for a heart stuck on idols: worship of the one real God.

When we have broken God's very first commandment, "I am the LORD your God. . . . You shall have no other gods before me" (Exod. 20:2–3), we can be sure the Lord wants to work a radical change inside us. Because we have let a desire swell into a consuming demand that rules our hearts, God wants to regain his rightful place at the core of our lives.

God doesn't whisk away all our idols in an instantaneous spiritual experience. Instead, he invites us to identify and confess our idols one by one and then cooperate with him as he removes them bit by bit from our hearts.

As you have read this chapter, maybe you have recognized idols you have allowed to dominate your heart—unmet desires at the root of many conflicts. Talk to God about those idols. Confess your wrongheaded worship. Accept his forgiveness. Then begin afresh to worship the one true God.

Here's how. If you want to squeeze the idols out of your heart and leave no room for them to return, make it your top priority to aggressively pursue an all-consuming worship of the living God. Ask him to teach you how to fear, love, trust, and delight in him more than anything in this world. The more you aim your heart at him, the less need you will feel to find happiness, fulfillment, or security in anything the world provides. You will toss away your idols, cling to God, and experience him more and more.

That is what began to happen the morning I (Ken) blew up at my children. I had been bowing before an idol of comfort and convenience. When I confessed my sin to my children and asked them to forgive my anger and harsh words, they responded with hugs of forgiveness and admitted that they too had been chasing idols that week. God reminded each of us that he is so much better than the idols we had allowed to dominate us. We were a few minutes late to church that morning, but our worship was more sincere, energized, and awe-filled than it had been for a long time.

Breaking Loose

He who conceals his sins does not prosper, but whoever confesses and renounces them finds mercy.

Proverbs 28:13

As a fire popped and crackled in the retreat center's massive stone fireplace, student after student stood before their youth group and confessed sins they had committed. Prompted by a message on the meaning of Jesus's death on the cross, they admitted to wrongs that included rebelling at home, gossip, jealousy, causing rifts in the group, and forming unwelcoming cliques at both church and school. As people opened up and shared their struggles, the room was awash with tears of joy and relief.

What caught everyone by surprise was Brent taking a turn at the front. Star receiver for the school's legendary football team, he was a guy who blamed everyone but himself when he dropped the ball. Now he was admitting all kinds of wrongs, recounting examples of his arrogance, and admitting that his desire to get a college scholarship had made him unconcerned about others. When Brent finished, he went straight to a teammate watching from the back of the room, where he did his best to apologize one-to-one for his past selfishness.

Peace with God, Peace with People

God's grace—his undeserved favor toward us—drives our peacemaking. Like Brent and the students in that youth group, we are motivated to make peace with others when we come face-to-face with the peace God has made with us through Jesus. The gospel reveals our awful sinfulness— nothing can save us except the death of God's only Son. It also reveals the depths of God's radical mercy—he gave his Son to die for us!

Jesus's death was the one act in all the universe that could bring us peace with God. He paid an infinite price for our sins. Rejected by his people and ridiculed by religious rulers, he was found guilty of crimes he didn't commit. He was mocked by fearsome soldiers who spit on him and beat him, pressing a crown of thorns into his head, wrapping his shoulders in a purple royal robe, and striking his skull with a staff they gave him as a king's scepter. Jesus's physical pain, however, was little compared to his spiritual pain. On the cross he bore the crushing weight of sin. Not *his* sin, because he had done no wrong. *Our* sin. As Isaiah 53:5 says, "He was pierced for our transgressions, he was crushed for our iniquities; the punishment that brought us peace was upon him, and by his wounds we are healed." This was an act of grace for our sake.

As we count on God's grace toward us, a couple of things happen. First, we let go of our pride, our defensiveness, and our illusions of how good we are. We honestly examine ourselves and break loose from the guilt and grip of sin. Second, we realize afresh how much reconciliation matters to God. His grace propels us to own our part of a conflict and do everything we can to mend relationships.

So exactly how does that repair process happen? It requires that we take four daring steps: *repentance, self-examination, confession,* and *change.*

Repentance Is More than a Feeling

Repentance is basic to who we are as Christians. It's the first step to breaking free from sin and conflict.

The word *repent* means to change the way we think. It means waking up to the fact that we have deceived ourselves and that our attitudes, ideas, values, or goals have been wrong. When this change in our thinking is real, it leads us to reject sin and turn to God for forgiveness and freedom. We can observe this process in Isaiah 55:7: "Let the wicked forsake his way and the evil man his thoughts. Let him turn to the LORD, and he will have mercy on him, and to our God, for he will freely pardon."

Repentance means far more than simply feeling sad or uncomfortable or embarrassed by what we have done. Although repentance often comes with sorrow and even tears, feeling awful doesn't prove we are repentant. In fact, there is a vast gap between normal human regret and authentic godly sorrow. Human sorrow just means feeling bad because we experience nagging guilt. Or because we got caught or have to endure unpleasant consequences. Or because we are embarrassed by a soiled reputation or the sheer stupidity of our actions.

Normal people feel regret when caught in that kind of squeeze. Before long their sorrow fades, however, and most people go back to doing what they did before. Instead of changing how they think and act, they simply try harder not to get caught.

I (Kevin) frequently hear parents say they don't want their teenagers to abuse alcohol. But I have heard some of those same parents laugh as they recount stories of partying their way through high school or college. They have never thoroughly changed their minds about their wrongdoing, and their halfhearted remorse puts them on the road to further grief. Their sons and daughters can't help but absorb that attitude.

Godly sorrow is utterly different. It means feeling bad because you have offended God. It entails sincerely regretting the fact that what you did was morally wrong, even if you don't have to suffer tough consequences. Authentic repentance involves a total change of heart. True repentance isn't always accompanied by intense feelings, but it always includes a change in thinking that leads to new behavior.

Examine Yourself

One proof that we have honestly repented is a willingness to look hard at ourselves and allow God to show us our sins. Few of us have developed a habit of identifying and confessing our wrongs, but here are three ways to start.

First, ask God to help you see your sin and repent of it. Pray the words of Psalm 139:23–24: "Search me, O God, and know my heart; test me and know my anxious thoughts. See if there is any offensive way in me, and lead me in the way everlasting." At first that prayer feels terrifying, but it powerfully reminds you that the God who sees you at your worst also loves you the most.

Second, ask a spiritually mature friend to help you spot your attitudes and patterns. Proverbs 19:20 teaches, "Listen to advice and accept instruction, and in the end you will be wise." The older I (Ken) get, the less I trust myself to be impartial about my part in a conflict. So I surround myself with family, friends, co-workers, and other spiritual partners who can openly critique my role in a conflict. I don't always like what these special people have to say, but when I humble myself and listen to their correction, they always help me see things more clearly.

Third, study God's Word to discern where your ways don't line up with God's. Some Christians have no idea what God expects because they don't know the Bible. They are missing an amazing opportunity to figure out life. Hebrews 4:12 alerts us that the Bible is razor-edged: "For the word of God is alive and powerful. It is sharper than the sharpest two-edged sword, cutting between soul and spirit, between joint and marrow. It exposes our innermost thoughts and desires" (NLT). If we want to discover God's way to live, Scripture is where we turn.

We are most likely to sin in our clashes with others in a few common ways. As you examine yourself to see your own contribution to a conflict, watch out for these areas.

Using Our Tongues as Weapons

Scripture warns us that our mouths can be a chief cause of conflict: "Consider what a great forest is set on fire by a small spark. The tongue also is a fire, a world of evil among the parts of the body. It corrupts the whole person. . . . It is a restless evil, full of deadly poison" (James 3:5–6, 8). We sin anytime our words violate God's high standard for talking to or about others: "Do not let any unwholesome talk come out of your mouths, but only what is helpful for building others up according to their needs, that it may benefit those who listen" (Eph. 4:29).

I (Kevin) mentioned in chapter 1 that getting control of my mouth was one of the main areas where God wanted me to grow when I began to follow Jesus wholeheartedly. I had developed such bad habits in how I talked to others that I needed a filter for my mouth. Ephesians 4:29 became my straightforward test of whether something was fit to say. I could ask myself, "Is this wholesome? Is it helpful? Does it build others up? Does it meet needs? Is it beneficial?" Many of my words failed that test. Yet identifying the problem put me on the way to a solution. I am still not perfect in what I say, but I no longer hurt others nonstop. I can see now that God was preparing me for a life full of words—writing, speaking, and counseling.

We misuse words in many ways. Our words might be reckless, like when we talk without thinking. Or our sin might be grumbling and complaining. Or falsehoods like lying, exaggerating, telling half-truths, distorting, or breaking promises. Often our gossiping both ignites and fuels a conflict. We gossip whenever we discuss unflattering details about a person with someone else who isn't part of the problem or its solution. Gossip is wrong even if the information is true. Slander goes a step further by speaking false, vicious words about another person.

If you see yourself in any of those descriptions, you can be sure your words contribute to conflict.

Controlling Others

Some people trigger conflict by constantly dominating others. Like puppeteers pulling strings, they manipulate siblings, peers, and even parents to serve their wishes.

Morgan has had the world wrapped around her finger since she was the cutest baby in the nursery. Youngest in her family by several years, she grew up with others waiting on her. Now in high school, she is quick to smile—or pout—to get her way. Her parents give her what she wants just to save themselves from having to endure yet another episode of out-of-control sulking.

Some attempts to control others are blatantly self-serving, like demanding our own comfort, popularity, or power at another's expense. More often we simply try to persuade, manipulate, or force people to do what we want, aiming to make our own lives better. Few things cause as much conflict as trying to control other people, and we don't have to be master puppeteers to be guilty of this wrong.

Failing to Respect Authority

For many young people, rebelling against authority is another major source of conflict. They revolt against the powers God has established in family, school, workplace, church, and government. As the Ruler above all other rulers, God has created legitimate authorities to maintain peace and order and has given those in authority strict commands not to take advantage of their position. Authorities should instead strive to watch out for the well-being of those they lead.

God commands us to submit to all forms of authority in our lives. While we might object to the idea of submitting to anyone, rebelling against biblically established authority is rebelling against God. Romans 13:2 puts it plainly: "He who rebels against the authority is rebelling against what God has instituted, and those who do so will bring judgment on themselves." As Christian author R. C. Sproul writes, "To say you honor the kingdom of Christ while you disobey his authority structure is to be guilty not only of hypocrisy but of cosmic treason."[1]

We can't choose to submit to authority only some of the time. In my last months of high school I (Kevin) protested to a teacher that I didn't want to read a brutally violent and sexually explicit novel that had been assigned for class. He allowed me to pick a different book. A few weeks later I cut school for senior skip day—a tradition not allowed by the school. The teacher, who was a fairly devout follower of another faith, was unimpressed by my disrespect for authority and my lack of consistent character. In a single day I undid the witness I had been attempting to build all year long.

Respect for authority is so important that Jesus commands us to submit to all leaders—good and bad, hypocritical and harsh. However, authority has limits. Since God hasn't given anyone the power to require us to sin, it's right to disobey any instructions that contradict the clear teaching of Scripture. When an authority commands us to do something we

81

believe is unwise, unfair, or sinful, we can respectfully try to persuade that person to do what is right. If our pleading doesn't cause that person to change course, we should obey any instructions that don't violate Scripture—and obey God in the rest, trusting the Lord to take care of the results.

Serving Sinful Desires

We saw in the last chapter that conflicts are often ignited by unmet desires that have gained control over our hearts. These consuming desires—idols of the heart—can take many forms. Lust can involve not only sexual immorality but also overeating, gambling, laziness, or other forms of self-indulgence. Pride can make us defensive, slow to admit our wrongs, deaf to advice, hot to win an argument, and quick to find fault with others. Love of money can tempt us to envy, lie, steal, or spend all our energy pursuing things we don't need. Fear of people can mean an actual dread of what others can do to us or an excessive concern about what others think of us, and either one can cause us to seek acceptance and popularity at any cost.

As we saw in the last chapter, some of the most tenacious idols we have to deal with are the good things we want too much, desires that we elevate to demands. Even healthy desires for love, respect, comfort, convenience, or success can cause horrible conflicts if we let them control our hearts.

Forgetting the Golden Rule

Probably the most common cause of conflict is simply our failure to follow the Golden Rule, which Jesus taught in Matthew 7:12: "So in everything, do to others what you would have them do to you." To see whether you have violated this teaching, ask yourself whether you want people to treat you the way you treat them. Or how you would feel if people said about you what you say about them. That is the standard Jesus gave us as one of the most important tests of everything we do and say.

The Seven A's of Confession

God cheers when you repent, choosing to flee evil and live his way. He loves it when you examine yourself to determine your part in a conflict. As God opens your eyes to see how you have sinned against others, he also wants to help you find freedom from your past wrongs. That happens through confession.

Many people never break loose and experience this amazing release because they never learn to admit their wrongs honestly and absolutely. When you were a little kid, it was a good first step to learn to apologize. But you no doubt sense the difference between a forced "I'm sorry" and a heartfelt "I did something wrong." Authentic confession means getting past cheap phrases like "I'm sorry if I hurt you," "Let's just forget it," and "I guess it's not all your fault." Mumbling those feeble words rarely brings people back together!

If you really want to make peace, ask God to help you breathe grace to others by humbly—and thoroughly—admitting your wrongs. One way to do this is to use what we call "the seven A's." Not every confession needs all seven steps. You can deal with minor offenses with a fairly simple statement. The more major the offense, however, the smarter you are to do a thorough confession using most or all of the seven A's.

1. Address Everyone Involved

Real confession begins by owning your sin to everyone directly impacted by your sin. Since every wrongdoing offends God, start your confession with him. Whether or not you admit a sin to other people depends on whether it was a "heart sin" or a "social sin." A heart sin takes place only in your thoughts and doesn't directly affect others, so it only needs to be confessed to God. A social sin involves other people. Confess those wrongs to anyone affected—a single individual or a group, people you hurt or who just witnessed your wrongdoing. The general rule? Your confession should reach as far as your offense.

2. Avoid If, But, and Maybe

The quickest way to wreck a confession is using words that shift the blame to others or minimize or excuse your guilt. The most common way to do this is to say, "I'm sorry if I've done something to make you mad." The word *if* ruins this confession, because it implies that you don't know whether you did something wrong. It sounds like you just want someone off your back. The same goes for *maybe*, as in, "Maybe I was the one who did it." Using the word *but* can completely undo a confession: "I know I'm hard to get along with, but I've been really tired lately." A confession is also canceled out if it has an excuse in it.

3. Admit Specifically

The more detail you provide when you confess, the more likely you are to get a positive reaction. Specific admissions help convince others that you are honestly facing up to what you have done, a signal that makes it far easier for them to forgive you. Not only that, but being specific helps you identify the actions, words, or attitudes you need to change. For example, instead of saying, "I blew it as a friend," you could say, "I know I hurt you when I talked behind your back."

4. Acknowledge the Hurt

If you want someone to respond positively to your confession, make it a point to express your sadness at the hurt you caused. Aim to show that you understand how the other person felt as a result of your words or actions. "You must have felt really embarrassed when I said those things in front of everyone. I'm so sorry I did that to you." If you aren't sure how the other person felt, ask and then acknowledge the hurt.

5. Accept the Consequences

Accepting any penalty your actions deserve is another way to demonstrate genuine repentance. You might have to earn back a person's trust. Or you might have to work extra to pay for damages you caused to someone's property. The harder you work to make restitution and repair any harm you have caused, the easier it is for others to trust your confession.

6. Alter Your Behavior

You don't really mean that you are sorry if you are planning on sinning again. Sincere repentance includes explaining to the person you offended how you plan to change in the future—what you'll say, how you'll act, or the attitude you'll display. Get specific. Find someone to hold you accountable. Explain that you are relying on God's help.

7. Ask for Forgiveness (and Allow Time)

If you talk through each of those steps with someone you have offended, often he or she will be willing to quickly forgive you and move on. If the person you have confessed to doesn't express forgiveness, however, you can ask, "Will you please forgive me?" Your question signals that you are now awaiting their move. Don't be surprised if some people need time to forgive you. Reconciliation doesn't always happen right away, and pressure from you won't help. If someone isn't ready to forgive you, make sure you have confessed thoroughly. If you sense that the person to whom you confessed is simply not ready to forgive you, it may be helpful to say something like this: "I know I hurt you, and I can understand why it might be hard to forgive me. I want us to be okay with each other, so I hope you can forgive me. In the meantime, I will pray for you and do my best to repair the damage I caused. With God's help, I will work to overcome my problem. If there's anything else I can do, please let me know."

You Can Change

When Brent stood before his youth group and talked about his arrogance and selfishness, his confession would have been meaningless if he then went back to the same old patterns. The same is true for each of us. The world is watching us with wide-open eyes, waiting to see if our attitudes, words, and actions live up to our confession.

As God works in you to deal with your part in a conflict, his goal isn't just to remove your guilt. He wants you to learn new behaviors that don't hurt others, dishonor him, or do injury to you. The final step in breaking free from any particular sin is working with God to bring about genuine personal change.

As you embark on this journey to change, you can be sure that God is eager to help you to grow and change. There is no sin or habit that can't be overcome by his grace. If you are a follower of Jesus, God has already given you a new mind and a new inner nature powered by his Holy Spirit, and he promises to continually work in you so that you can learn to replace your old sinful behaviors with his new habits.

Your youth group or other Christian friends can help you enormously on this trip. On the way, you will want to make the most of your Bible to change your thinking and point you down the right path. You will want to pray for God's strength daily. You will want to aim your heart at God, learning to love him with your whole being. And you will need to keep in mind that new ways of doing life take practice. Situation after situation will test your commitment to living God's way. But with God's help and disciplined practice, you can develop a Christlike character that proves your repentance for everyone to see—and lets you enjoy the benefits of peace.

G3: GENTLY RESTORE

Brothers, if someone is caught in a sin, you who are spiritual should restore him gently.

Galatians 6:1

Friends ever since they sat next to each other on the story rug back in kindergarten, Scott and Kailee could still get on each other's nerves—like when Scott teased Kailee about being an airhead. She was plenty smart, but she knew as well as everyone else that her mouth frequently moved before her mind was fully engaged.

In small doses Scott's teasing made Kailee laugh, and she could easily share in the humor of what popped unfiltered from her brain. Yet sometimes the teasing hit Kailee sideways. She could enjoy Scott's joking as long as it stayed between the two of them, but when Scott called attention to her mess-ups in front of other people, she faked laughter, ducked away, and avoided him for days. Because Kailee never brought up how much his teasing hurt, Scott continued to experience mindless moments of his own, unintentionally humiliating a friend without noticing what he was doing.

Enough Is Enough

Sometimes you immediately know that you can't let go of a wrong because a single action is too awful to overlook. At other times a fault might play out again and again, so that sooner or later you realize that minor actions are adding up to major relationship damage. Either way, you reach a point where the hurt causes you to say, "Enough is enough!" You sense that the time for overlooking a fault is past. You need to do something. Knowing that you need to act, however, isn't the same as knowing exactly what to do.

In eighth grade I (Kevin) spotted a friend exiting phys ed with an arm that looked liked a bent coat hanger sculpture. From his wrist to his elbow, Andrew's limb was twisted at angles not normally found in nature. When I saw Andrew's serious injury and dazed look, it never occurred to me to pretend a problem didn't exist. Nor did I parade Andrew through the school hallways, as if making sure that everyone got a good look at his multiple fractures was the chief concern of the moment. Rather, I quickly took the simple steps we all learn in health class. I told Andrew to hold still, found the school nurse, and helped him out as he healed. (And no, I never figured out how he slipped past the phys ed teacher looking like he did.)

Yet suppose you spotted a friend troubled not by an obvious physical injury but by a clear moral or spiritual breakage. Someone "caught in a sin," as Galatians 6:1 puts it. Not just "caught" as in "discovered doing wrong" or "tangled once or twice," but "stuck," "trapped," or "snared" by evil. Picture a friend or acquaintance who has a habit of causing pain to you, to others, or to himself or of showing dishonor toward God.

Suddenly the right response might not feel as obvious as helping a friend with a broken arm. We might stammer, stall, and stumble trying to formulate a plan. It's much harder to act than to think of reasons to ignore the problem. We might assume that the issue will solve itself without any effort on our part. We might fear that our addressing the situation will be interpreted as moral or spiritual superiority and that whatever we say or do will come off as judgmental and arrogant. Or we might mistakenly decide that the highly practical biblical principle of overlooking—deliberately letting a wrong go—covers every evil situation we face. Any one of these thoughts can cause us to walk away without attempting to solve a conflict.

Living *Katartizo*

The Bible offers us a better solution, a call to daring relationships in which we deal directly with the person doing wrong, working to resolve the problem by acting on clear strategies outlined in God's Word.

In Galatians 6:1 the apostle Paul actually uses a medical term to describe this intentional response to wrongdoing. He writes, "If someone is caught in a sin, you who are spiritual should restore him gently." The Greek word for "restore," *katartizo*, literally means "to set a broken bone." When you *katartizo* the people in your world, you do the best you can to help them. You might cause pain in the short term, like the emergency room doctor tasked with aligning the bones in Andrew's forearm. But you don't inflict lasting misery. By helping others see their failings and take responsibility for their wrong actions, your loving care prevents a part of their life from being forever bent out of shape. Helping others identify and find healing for their faults can be the ultimate act of servanthood.

Notice in Galatians 6:1 that key phrases appear before and after Paul's words about restoration. The beginning of the verse cautions that it takes spiritual maturity to be truly helpful to someone caught in sin. Don't equate that requirement with spiritual perfection, or we would all have yet another reason never to get involved in others' lives. The kind of maturity you need is a strong commitment to Christ so that you don't get dragged into whatever sin has trapped the person you aim to help. Those words of warning also assume that you are acting on the first two G's of peacemaking—that before you attempt to help others own their part of a conflict, you have deliberately put God's glory first and are working to get the log out of your own eye. The end of the verse also says that genuine restoration requires you to deal gently with people stuck in evil. While you need to approach them with the firm strength of Christlike love, you don't use it as an opportunity to attack them any more than you would flog a broken bone.

Talking to people about their shortcomings might sound complicated and even terrifying. Yet the steps in God's strategy can become as straightforward and second nature to you as mastering basic first aid skills. You will feel confident with the relational equivalent of a scrape or small cut. You will even store up wisdom to be a helpful first responder when you encounter relatively rare situations as dire as a gushing wound, plugged airway, or stopped heart. We have no doubt that as you practice God's principles of peacemaking, you will learn to stay calm, skillfully get the job done, and help yourself and others experience the awesome relationships God created us to enjoy.

Just between Us

If your brother sins against you, go and show him
his fault, just between the two of you.

Matthew 18:15

Alicia, Brook, and Emily were crazed with anticipation as
they looked forward to what they had dubbed "The Year of
the Driver's License." With all three old enough to get their
provisional cards, it would be good-bye parental-driven car-
pools, hello sweet freedom.

Since their birthdays were staggered throughout the year,
Emily passed her behind-the-wheel test many months before
the other girls. Once she survived her mom and dad's additional month-long trial of driving alone with no mishaps,
Alicia and Brook had permission from all three sets of parents to finally ride along with her. So Emily drove to Bible
study . . . the mall . . . movies . . . everywhere.

At first things went according to the agreement the girls
had worked out long before. Because Emily drove, Alicia

and Brook happily helped pay for gas. When the two girls also earned their licenses, however, they stopped chipping in. Emily still drove almost all the time, but now Alicia and Brook reasoned that she was in the driver's seat because she chose to be, not because they had to have a ride. So they bluntly told Emily she could fill her own tank. A few days later when Emily silently handed her friends a detailed list of all the places she had driven, her mileage, and what they owed her, they weren't exactly persuaded of her point.

Why Go and Show?

We all know people who are all about being up front with those who wrong them. As we watch them stomp toward their offenders, it might seem like they are applying some well-known advice of Jesus: "If your brother sins against you, go and show him his fault, just between the two of you" (Matt. 18:15). But simply getting in the face of those who wrong us doesn't cover what Jesus wants us to do.

If you read that verse all by itself, you might assume that Jesus wants you to catch people being bad, confront them directly, and force them to admit they have sinned. If you check the context of that verse, however, you see that Jesus had in mind something far more flexible and helpful than going nose-to-nose with others to rattle off a list of their faults and tell them how to behave. Jesus cares less about our need for justice than about the person who needs help.

To get the whole meaning, you have to look back to Jesus's enlightening metaphor of a loving shepherd who tracks down a wandering sheep, rejoices when he finds it, and returns it to the flock where it can receive his constant, tender attention. That point comes in Matthew 18:12–14, so what Jesus says in verse 15 about talking to others about their sin actually comes midstream in his message. When you realize this, it is clear that he is teaching us to rescue people from their sin, not rub their faces in it. Moreover, right after instructing us to "go and show him his fault," he hits this restoration theme again by adding, "If he listens to you, you have won your brother over" (v. 15). In case all of that still isn't loud and clear enough, he hits his point a third time by telling a parable about an unmerciful servant who fails to extend to others the compassion that he had received (see Matt. 18:21–35).

Can you see that the purpose of going and showing someone a fault is to imitate Jesus's shepherd love? Your job is not to hunt down evildoers to make them meet your demands but instead to rescue them from sin and restore them to relationship with God and anyone they have offended.

When You Shouldn't Let It Go

We have said that overlooking—letting go of a wrong done to you—is a peacemaker's first option in responding to conflict. It's the choice to consider before you take any other steps to address a tense situation, because overlooking insignificant offenses creates an atmosphere of grace in everyday life. It's how we can let go of small hurts and move on with life.

But overlooking isn't the only option. In fact, it can be the wrong option. Used inappropriately, overlooking becomes a peacefaking ploy that allows evil to persist and spread. At that point, to skillfully "go and show"—talking one-on-one with a person about his or her contribution to a conflict—is the right way to find a solution.

While it's sometimes tough to decide whether an offense is serious enough to go and show, several signs can indicate that a problem is creating enough harm that you can't let it slide. Note that a situation doesn't have to exhibit all of these signs to be too serious to overlook. Any one of these signals can be important enough to require action.

The Offense Dishonors God

The apostle Paul spoke up about sin when the failings of religious leaders of his day made God's followers look foolish to their pagan society (see Rom. 2:23–24). Peter told us to live such good lives among nonbelievers that they can readily spot God's glory in us (see 1 Peter 2:12). So if someone who claims to be a Christian acts in a way that causes others to mock God, his people, or his Word, you might need to talk with that person and urge him to change his behavior. This doesn't mean that you should point out every little misstep, because God himself patiently puts up with much of what we do wrong. But when someone's sin obviously and negatively impacts how others see God, it needs to be addressed.

I (Kevin) have found that students can be in a unique position to spot when actions blatantly dishonor God. As a youth pastor, for instance, I had students pull me aside to tell me in confidence that a married adult volunteer was having an affair, a situation I otherwise had no way of knowing about. Others knew when a peer was partying hard on Saturday night and leading worship on Sunday morning. Telling me these facts wasn't tattling. It was the first step in getting help for these individuals; they needed assistance in repairing serious compromises of integrity that could cause Christians to stumble in their faith and non-Christians to be turned off to Christianity. God doesn't tell you to serve him as a spy, but you often see into areas that adults can't. You can help keep others accountable.

The Offense Damages Your Relationship

You should also go and show when an offense damages your relationship with another person. Every offense affects the way you get along with someone, but if your feelings, thoughts, words, or actions toward another person have been altered for more than a short period of time, then the offense is probably too serious to let go.

While Emily could have used a whole lot more sensitivity and style in presenting her concerns about driving to Alicia and Brook, she knew her feelings about the situation weren't quickly fading. From her point of view, her friends had broken an explicit agreement. If the three girls didn't talk about the situation, they would stay mad at each other. This relatively small conflict could even end their friendship. Yet a simple discussion would have the potential to uncover a workable solution, like each person taking turns driving from now on. Rather than letting her own frustration build further, Emily was smart enough to bring the problem to her friends' attention so a hurtful pattern could be changed.

This point is intensely practical. How many friends are no longer a part of your life because a conflict—maybe petty, maybe significant—left you distant from each other? Countless human relationships wouldn't be strained or permanently severed if one person had initiated an honest conversation to sort out the disagreement.

The Offense Hurts You or Others

This one isn't as obvious as it sounds, because the hurts caused by your conflicts are often more subtle than a playground fight involving punching or pulling hair. The damages that result can also be more far-reaching.

The harm in any conflict, of course, can be direct, a sort of verbal or emotional punch straight to the gut, either yours or someone else's. When that pain lingers, you probably need to go and show the offender what has happened.

But the negative impact of a conflict can also be harder to see, multiplying indirectly to a larger network. An offender might set an example that encourages others to behave badly. In this case Paul commands Christians to address open sin quickly to keep other believers from being led down the wrong path (see 1 Cor. 5:6). Or a conflict can ruin many lives if it forces people to pick sides. It's not difficult to picture everyday examples in which a small personal disagreement mushrooms into a mob riot—probably not an actual group-on-group street fight but a conflict that begins to split a family, school, church, or crowd of friends. You are unwise to let that slide.

Take the case of the partying worship leader, for example. Because the situation wasn't dealt with swiftly, what began as an individual issue of dishonoring God began to harm a large student population. A sizable group of peers took offense at this person's behavior and dismissed the church as hypocritical. Left uncorrected, the situation could poison the unity that God intends for the church—a tight community that demonstrates his existence and love for all to see.

The Offense Hurts the Offender

Here's where we likely have the toughest time seeing a reason to intervene and help someone understand their role in a conflict. After all, without God's power working in us, our natural bent is to punish people who cause us pain, not make sure they get help!

It also can be difficult for us to dissect this part of a conflict. Put yourself back in Emily's position. She no doubt feels her kindness was taken for granted. She's also short on cash. So what possible harm came to Alicia and Brook? Not only do they seem at peace with their actions, but with their combined savings and intact friendship, they can hit a drive-through for a couple of premium lattes.

Our limited human perspective keeps us from seeing how Alicia and Brook are being hurt. As Christians we are interconnected parts of a body, so doing anything that damages a relationship is like banging our own thumb with a hammer. In other words, the pain we cause others is really pain we cause ourselves. Also, Alicia and Brook may know they broke

Christian Confrontation

The Bible clearly teaches that it's not okay to let people continue on destructive paths. These verses are worth posting in your locker:

> *Rescue those who are unjustly sentenced to die; save them as they stagger to their death. Don't excuse yourself by saying, "Look, we didn't know." For God understands all hearts, and he sees you. He who guards your soul knows you knew. He will repay all people as their actions deserve.*
> *Proverbs 24:11–12 NLT*

> *My brothers and sisters, if one of you wanders away from the truth, and someone helps that person come back, remember this: Anyone who brings a sinner back from the wrong way will save that sinner's soul from death and will cause many sins to be forgiven.*
> *James 5:19–20 NCV*

These Bible instructions that tell us to go and show others their faults aren't an excuse to run from person to person looking for opportunities to point out sin. In fact, if you gush with enthusiasm to point out others' failings, you are likely not up to the job. That kind of eagerness displays a pride and spiritual immaturity that devastates our ability to genuinely minister to others. The world's best confronters are usually people who would rather avoid the job but go and show out of obedience to God and love for others.

a promise to Emily; they may sense that they have violated their consciences. And in the end, any wrongdoing distances us from God and potentially leads us to further destruction.

So Alicia and Brook have not only offended Emily, they have hurt themselves—and they need help.

In some instances people do more obvious damage to themselves that extends to others, like substance abuse, rebellion, or sexual immorality. Sometimes the immediate, short-term damage appears to be limited to the individual, like cutting, wallowing in bitterness, or staring at pornography. But whatever the source or reach of the hurt, being a follower of Jesus means looking out for the well-being of other Christians—especially people in your own family, those in your church, or close friends—is a major responsibility. It's distressing that many Christians take the standard view that we should let everyone "do their own thing." Some believers do nothing even when they see a brother or sister in Christ trapped in serious sin. This isn't the kind of love Jesus showed.

One More Reason to Go

We realize that the idea of going to others to help them own their part of a conflict might sound tough. So in the next two chapters we will give you specific guidance on talking to people who have wronged—ways that give you the best possible chance of a good outcome. We also want to explain your options when things go wrong, because not everyone responds well to even the most calm and kind confrontation. But while you chew on the idea of going and showing, we want to tell you one more story about a time when God said to initiate a conversation in the midst of conflict.

Back in college I (Ken) sensed that a friend was treating me strangely at church. This guy—I'll call him Brad—used to be easy to talk to and joke around with, but our conversations had suddenly turned cold and formal. No more laughing like we usually did. Brad was suddenly very deliberate and serious around me.

Assuming he was struggling at home or work, I asked him how he was doing. Brad brushed my question aside with a cool "I'm fine," then moved on to talk with others in the church lobby. As I watched them talk, I noticed that Brad had switched back to his old self, kidding around with them like he used to do with me. When I saw that he was his usual self as he interacted with several other people, I realized that I was the only person getting brushed off.

All that week I was haunted by a feeling that Brad was upset with me. Hard as I tried, I couldn't think of anything I had said or done that might have offended him. As I drove to church the next Sunday, I hoped Brad would be back to normal. No way. When I greeted him before Sunday school, his face dropped into that same cool look. *Oh great!* I thought. *He's really mad at me, and I don't have a clue why.* I didn't hear a word our pastor taught. I kept sifting through the last few weeks to see if I could recall anything I had done that might have angered Brad. Still nothing.

I couldn't catch Brad after church, so I drove home still bothered by the gap that had opened between us. By midafternoon I couldn't take the suspense any longer. I walked to Brad's dorm and knocked on his door. When he opened the door and saw me, his natural smile was once again replaced by ice.

"I'm sorry to barge in," I began. "But if you have just a few minutes, I'd really appreciate being able to talk with you." His hesitation said it all. He didn't want to talk, but he was too polite to just tell me to go away.

"Brad, I can tell something isn't right between us," I continued. "Let me come in so we can work this out. You've always been a good friend, and if I've done something to offend you, I really want to know what it is so I can make things right between us."

Brad's expression softened a bit as he opened the door wider and said, "Okay."

The next few minutes were awkward. I probed for a reason why Brad was so cool toward me, and he tried to pretend like it was no big deal. After a while he finally told me that I had deeply embarrassed him by a comment I had made about something he said in Sunday school. As soon as he recounted the words I had meant as a joke, I could see why they had hurt him. I sincerely apologized for speaking in such a mindless and hurtful way and for embarrassing him in front of our friends. Even though my confession wasn't very thorough—I didn't think about committing to change or offering to admit my wrong to our friends—Brad smiled at me.

Brad joked that he would have to give up his plans to embarrass me in class, then asked if I wanted to go grab a burger. I thought that anything would be better than another night of dorm food. As we headed down the hallway, I said, "Just to make it up to you, I'm buying."

"If that's the case," he responded, "you can embarrass me any time you want. A free meal more than makes up for a little humiliation." The world was back to normal.

My experience with Brad was one of the first times I learned the benefit of going to someone to try to make peace. I realized that I needed to take the first step even when I didn't think I had done anything to cause the problem. Jesus says this duty is so important that we should stop in our tracks—even as we worship—and go reconcile with anyone who holds a grudge against us (see Matt. 5:23–24). Whether or not a charge against us seems to be true, we need to take responsibility for going and seeking peace.

I've never forgotten how following God's ways can repair a friendship.

Exceptions to the Rule

Now that we have told you how immensely important it is for you to go firsthand to an offender when it isn't appropriate to overlook an offense, we need to inform you of a couple exceptions to that general rule. In some situations someone besides you needs to go and show.

The first situation is when it seems wise to use a go-between at the beginning. This isn't a chance to send a bully to fight your battles or a friend to shuttle back and forth making deals like a Middle East diplomat. But there are instances in which someone close to you knows an offender far better than you do. That close friend might effectively raise the issue with the person who hurt you and offer to set up a meeting. The point is that you still work toward a face-to-face conversation.

The second exception is a much stronger caution. As a young person you should never face some situations by yourself. While it's essential that you learn to respectfully appeal to adults with whom you clash, some adults operate with such power and intimidation that it isn't wise to try to navigate that type of conflict on your own. We urge you to send a responsible representative in your place, whether it is an older friend, a parent, a pastor, or a teacher. This warning is even more important in situations such as abuse. If you or a friend has endured physical, emotional, or sexual abuse from a person, it isn't your job or any young person's job to face that person alone and risk further harm. Get an adult on your side—and, if appropriate, involve a counselor or police officer.

Your Chance to Serve

As you ponder everything we have shared in this chapter, remember this astonishing truth: every conflict presents you with a one-of-a-kind opportunity to serve others. Your clash might put you in a prime location to offer helpful advice, demonstrate a positive example, or even suggest imaginative solutions to problems. When you notice people buried by various issues or stressed to the point of exploding, God can use you to help them. And one of the best ways you can help others in the midst of conflict is by helping them see areas where they need to change. At the start, that step can feel unbelievably tough. But when you go and show, you will often see the person you talk to—as well as your relationship with that person—make enormous strides.

Speak Truth—
but Listen First

Speaking the truth in love, we will in all things grow
up into him who is the Head, that is, Christ.

Ephesians 4:15

All of my life I (Kevin) have loudly admitted my lack of co-ordination. As a soccer coach once accurately put it, I am "all aggress and no finesse." So with warm parental pride, my wife and I have smiled as our children have each thrown themselves into various demanding winter sports. Our daughter Karin has focused on alpine skiing, a sport I have carefully avoided since my older sister overshot the end of a ski run, crashed into a parked car, and came home in a leg cast.

This past winter my daughter's team was on the local hill—there are no mountains in Minnesota—for a routine after-school practice. During practice the guys' captain, Jeff, snagged his ski on a gate during a run he had made thousands of times before. Slicing down the hill at more than fifty miles an hour, he instantly stopped, pivoted, and slammed his head into the icy snow. Despite the protection of his helmet, his body wracked with convulsions.

No one minimized the seriousness of Jeff's fall. The ski patrol loaded him onto a snow stretcher and lowered him off the hill. Paramedics sped him away in an ambulance. Technicians carefully moved him into place for an MRI. Nurses tended him. Doctors studied him, interpreted his test results, and prescribed a regimen to get him back on the hill.

Jeff was in a bad spot. As he came back to his senses there was, for a while, little that we non-medical types could do for him. What really counted at that time were the words spoken to him. What he didn't need were harsh, condemning, hopeless words, like "You must be stupid racing down a rutted slope," or "You shouldn't be skiing at all," or "I know someone who had an accident like this and didn't recover." Jeff needed words to lift him up and get him back on the hill.

Your All-Important Words

Whenever you have the chance to restore a person who has tumbled into sin, your words can make or break the outcome. The tongue, after all, is like a tiny rudder that makes a huge ship turn one way or another (see James 3:4–5). Speak badly and you widen the rift between yourself and your opponent. Speak well and you have a shot at pulling the relationship back together. If your words seem to do more harm than good when you try to resolve a disagreement, don't give up. With God's help you can improve your ability to communicate constructively in any go-and-show encounter.

We want to give you some basic principles and skills for productive conversations, grouped according to the time you will need them—*before* you go and *as* you go. Each pointer is vitally important, but one or two might strike you as particularly crucial to apply in any specific conflict. So much of everyday peacemaking happens at this go-and-show stage that you can also look at these points as a long-term checklist of key skills to master. Each time you face a fresh conflict, pick a point to intentionally work on.

Before You Go

Surprisingly, you will find that much of what you need to do when you go and show actually happens before you ever open your mouth. Don't rush through this preparation process.

Pray for Love

Suppose you entered a go-and-show conversation the way I (Kevin) played fullback in soccer—charging left and right, slide-tackling the opponent, utilizing my size as my biggest asset. When it comes to *futbol*, that is part of the backfield defensive game. Yet my aggression entirely lacked the finely tuned moves that would put a ball in the goal.

Go-and-show encounters are like that. If you try to resolve a conflict by rushing the offender and terrifying them into submission, you lack the finesse it takes to really make peace. You might communicate a few facts about how you think and feel, but you clearly are missing the more important skill: love. God commands us not only to tell each other the truth when we have been wronged but also to say it all with love. That applies even when we face off with people who stare us down like an arch-rival team, such as those who have harshly wronged or mistreated us.

"Speaking the truth in love" (Eph. 4:15) begins long before the conversation, when you ask God to put a love into your heart that isn't naturally there. Ask him to give you the ability to communicate his love by speaking with patient gentleness and by acting with authentic concern for the other person's interests and well-being. Remember, your task is to show others the same shepherd love God never stops showing you.

Of course, there is a time for firm—even blunt—words, especially if an offender snubs your gentle approach and keeps on sinning. Even so, it's smart to start mellow and get stronger only if necessary. Strong words often trigger antagonism, and once a conversation goes there, it's tough to bring it back to a friendlier place.

Take a Bath

People with whom you clash can smell your attitude a long way away. So before you make an approach, you need to freshen up with a plunge in God's grace. I (Ken) know that when people disappoint or offend me, my first reaction is to lay down the law, lecturing them about how they have messed up and what they should now do to make things right. I'm really excellent at this. My children thank me all the time for my exceptionally clear explanations. Okay, actually, you might correctly guess that this tactic usually makes my kids and anyone else reluctant to admit their wrongs.

God is working to teach me a better way to approach others about their failures. Before I get near them, I soak in his grace—his kindness that I in no way deserve. I study his Book, worship him, pray, think about his goodness, and thank him for forgiving every one of my failings through the cross. Once I have plunged deep into God's grace, I can go to others smelling like a new man. Instead of focusing solely on how they have hurt me, I am able to confess my own wrongs, gently bring up their faults, and forgive them as God has forgiven me. I can talk about what Jesus has done and is doing daily for us. Preparing myself in this way makes people far more likely to listen to my concerns.

Assume the Best

If people sense that you have jumped to conclusions about them and enjoy finding fault in them, they will think it's pointless to talk to you. If instead they sense that you want to believe the best about them, they will be far more likely to listen to your concerns. So before you go, ask God to help you assume the best about others. You can choose to believe good things about others until facts prove otherwise. You can also choose not to see every disagreement in terms of good or bad, right or wrong, sin or righteousness. Recall that many offenses result from misunderstandings rather than actual wrongs. Others are all about personal preferences. Try if at all possible to see a disagreement at this level, and you won't come ready to execute moral judgment on your opponent.

Plan the Right How, When, and Where

Pop stars might dump their ex-loves with a text message, but you can do better. As you work to resolve a conflict, the time, place, and method of communication all matter.

No matter what type of conflict you face, you are doomed to a bad conversation if you discuss sensitive topics with someone who is tired, worried, or in a bad mood. It also won't go well if you don't have enough time to talk thoroughly about an important issue. And no one processes well in a place packed with distractions like TV, loud music, or crowds of people. Find a private yet safe place to talk.

As easy as it might be to make your point through a text message, email, note, or phone call, a face-to-face conversation is still the best way to resolve conflict, because then both people can see facial expressions, read body language, and hear words. You will get your full message across, and you will have the chance to clarify any misunderstandings.

Plan Your Words

As a pastor I (Kevin) have tough conversations all the time. I often need to lead my staff to consensus on complicated issues. I have to cover details that easily slip from my mind. At times I confront people or help them through tragic circumstances. And I rarely go into a discussion without prepared notes to guide me. My notes give me a basic script to start the conversation and keep me on topic. Writing them forces me to anticipate objections. When you need to talk with others about their faults, carefully planning your words can make the difference between peace and hostility. God thinks that planning ahead is a good idea: "Those who plan what is good find love and faithfulness" (Prov. 14:22).

In small matters it's fine to have an off-the-cuff chat, unless your brain is prone to off-the-top offensive remarks. When you need to deal with significant issues or sensitive people, however, think ahead of time about what you will say. Not the mean things you wish you could say but points that will move the situation to a solution. You can actually write notes about several things: the core issue you need to address, words that sum up your feelings, a description of the impact the problem has on you and others, suggestions for solving the problem, and the benefits of finding a solution. While it might unnerve people to see you approach with notes in hand, it also shows that you care so much about your conversation that you planned ahead.

Persuade—Don't Punish

When the Bible talks about how to best approach others to point out their faults, nowhere does it use words like "smash," "trounce," "verbally pummel," or "squeeze until your opponent cries." True, restoration might require direct confrontation, yet the Bible teaches that there are better ways to approach people than simply launching in and describing their wrongs. Scripture, in fact, rarely uses words we would translate as "confront" to describe the process of talking to others about their faults. Instead, it offers us a wide range of ways to help others. God's Word tells us to "confess," for example, or "teach," "instruct," "reason with," "show," "encourage," "correct," "warn," "admonish," or "rebuke." In providing all of these options, God allows us to adjust the intensity of our communication to fit the other person's position and the urgency of the situation.

Obviously, there is more to restoring others than simply confronting them with their wrongs. So before you go, ask God for wisdom. Ponder the question "How would I want to be approached about this issue?" Then run with the best idea God gives you.

As You Go

Having done all of this careful preparation before you go and show, you might assume your next move is to go . . . and show. As you approach someone to point out their wrongs, however, your first task isn't to talk. It's to listen.

Listen First!

Whenever I (Kevin) need to talk to students who are acting up at a youth group function, I assume I'm not the first person to have chatted with them about their attitude or behavior. Students have keenly honed responses to authority figures like principals, counselors, teachers, police, bosses, and parents. Anything I do to put students on the defensive won't help me get them on board with whatever the group is supposed to be doing.

So I start by doing something few authority figures seem to do in approaching unruly youth. I listen. I find a comfortable spot—often on the floor, so I don't loom over them—and I give them my full and unruffled attention. I work through a mental script where I ask them about what's happening, how they feel about it, and what they could do about it. I give them all the time they need, and in the course of the conversation I weave in my take on what's happening, how I feel about it, and what I think they could do about it. But never before I have heard them out.

The result of doing what seems like a highly *non*confrontational process is that most students get the point and begin to do exactly what they are supposed to do. Well, closer to what they are supposed to do. Instead of quitting the group because I get after them, they come back and bring their friends. Listening opens the door that lets me say tough things, and those tough things bring life change.

While I learned by example from my dad much of what I know about working with youth—he was an inner-city schoolteacher for thirty years—I am actually putting into practice some wise words from Scripture: "He who answers before listening—that is his folly and his shame" (Prov. 18:13). Or this: "My dear brothers and sisters: You must all be quick to listen, slow to speak, and slow to get angry. Human anger does not produce the righteousness God desires" (James 1:19–20 NLT). Fast ears. Slow mouth. Controlled emotions. It works.

Pay Attention

Most people have two good ears, but excellent listening is actually a communication and psychological science with known skills you can readily master.

How are your listening skills? Check the statement that best describes you:

___ I wait patiently while others talk.

___ I jump in and interrupt others.

By *waiting* you can get to the root cause of a conflict. By speaking before listening you break a person's train of thought, complicate the conversation, and tend to offer solutions prematurely. Get comfortable with silence, and discipline yourself to not interrupt others when they speak.

___ I give others my full attention when I listen.

___ I let my mind wander or plan what I want to say next.

By *attending* you take control of your brain, which can think at least a blazing four times faster than a person can talk. If you don't give others your full attention, you miss key points. They see your distraction and shut down. So you can attend to others by keeping regular eye contact—no evil-eye stare-downs, though—and avoiding bad body language like foot tapping, folding your arms, or looking around. Lean forward, nod your head, don't have a glum face, and occasionally insert a "hmmm," "uh-huh," "I see," or "oh" to keep others talking.

___ I ask questions when I don't understand what others mean.

___ I assume that I understand perfectly what people communicate.

By *clarifying* you make sure you grasp what the other person is saying. You can get the additional information you need by asking questions, "Can you give me an example?" or making statements like, "Tell me more about . . ." "I'm confused about . . ." and "Let me see if I understand . . ." Words like these show that you are hearing and thinking about what is being said. Clarifying what you don't understand gets you more and deeper information.

___ I can accurately sum up what others have said.

___ I don't track what others are saying closely enough to be able to say their points in my own words.

By *reflecting* you sum up the key thoughts and feelings of others and let them know you understand. A few classic ways to say this are: "What you're saying is . . ." "You believe that . . ." "So you were feeling like . . ." and "From your perspective you think that . . ." Reflecting doesn't mean you agree with others, just that you have listened and processed what they are saying. It shows that you are paying attention, focuses the conversation, and slows things down when emotions get heated. Moreover, if you listen to others, they are more likely to listen to you.

___ I try to find common ground even in hostile conversations.

___ I never agree on any point with those I oppose.

By *agreeing* with another person, you find common ground before you address your disagreements. Like other good listening habits, agreeing encourages further communication by breaking down hostility. It's especially important when you have been in the wrong. You will find that you stop arguing and start dialoguing when you honestly say things like "You're right. I was wrong when I . . ." "You know, a lot of what you just said is true . . ." "I can understand why you were upset when I . . ." Don't say you agree if you don't agree, but watch for areas where you don't have to fight.

Hopefully you can see that good listening can bring break-throughs in communication, and here's why: chances are that any issue you raise with someone isn't fresh news. Take the friend who habitually ignores your wishes and steers you toward whatever he or she wants to do. Others have been snapped by that selfishness for a long time. The teacher whose explanations of geometry totally lose you? Others have been puzzled for years. The sibling who mouths off to you? You know firsthand this has been a long-term problem. However, you can be the person who finally makes a differ-ence in those lives when you go and show—provided you listen first. By having fast ears, a slow mouth, and controlled emotions, you will avoid backing people into a corner, dem-onstrate that you don't have all the answers and need their side of the story, and demonstrate the personal interest God has in each one of us. Even when you can't agree with every-thing others say or do, your willingness to listen proves your respect and opens up communication.

Speak Up!

Somewhere in the course of a conversation you will sense that it is your turn to talk—after you have listened well, of course. So make your points well. Let's look at some im-portant skills.

Use "I" Statements

Over the years I (Ken) have learned from my wife, Cor-lette, the highly useful skill of using "I" statements. Many people who muster the courage to talk to others about their faults go on the attack using "You" statements like "You are so insensitive" or "You are totally selfish." It's far better to offer information about yourself using phrases that start with "I," like "I feel hurt when you . . ." or "I feel ignored when you . . ." You can even put the details into a formula: "I feel _____ when you _____, because _____. As a result _____." Roll that together and you get something like "I feel hurt when you make fun of me in front of other people, because it makes me feel stupid. As a result, I'm not sure I should hang out with you when other people are around."

Use "I" statements to tell a person how he or she affects you, specifically name the offense, and explain why the issue matters. The more another person understands your concerns and the impact their behavior has on you, the more willing they might be to deal with the problem.

Be Factual

When you go to point out faults, it's tempting to use phrases like "You always . . ." or "You never . . ." But people and circumstances are usually more complicated than that, a mix of good and not-so-good. Those remarks not only heat up a conversation but, if they exaggerate the situation, also reduce the likelihood that the other person will hear the rest of what you say. Try these swaps: Instead of "You always break your promises," say, "Three times in the past two weeks you have said you wanted to get together, but you've blown me off." Or instead of "I'm really tired of you never doing your share of our group projects," say, "I won't do this whole project. I need you to do a fair part of the work."

Use the Bible Carefully

The Bible might be totally on your side in a disagreement, and it can be a useful source of undeniable truth when you experience conflict with another Christian. If you bring in the Bible carelessly, however, you will alienate people rather than persuade them. It's not likely to help at all with non-Christians. When you talk to people who are not convinced of the Bible's authority, you can appeal to general principles of right and wrong. But the point is the same: watch how you do it!

Make sure your use of the Bible, like all other words you speak, meets the Ephesians 4:29 test: "When you talk, do not say harmful things, but say what people need—words that will help others become stronger. Then what you say will do good to those who listen to you" (NCV). When you want to use the Bible, if possible, let the other person read the passage from their own Bible and invite them to say what they think it means. And when using the Bible becomes a hindrance to a conversation, back off and give the other person time to consider its truth before you share more.

Get Feedback

Think about what we have said so far. To do the go-and-show task well, you do prep work. You listen. You start to speak. But even then you aren't done listening. While you might have eloquently described every last feeling and thought of your inner self, you have done no good if the other person doesn't comprehend what you have said.

In the same way that you clarified and reflected as you listened, invite the other person to talk about what he or she has heard you say. If this feedback hasn't come naturally in the course of your conversation, ask gently but directly with words like these: "I'm not sure I've said this clearly. Would you mind telling me what you think I've said?" "Have I confused you?" "What are you thinking about all this?" "What have I said that you agree with? What do you disagree with?"

Talk Solutions

As you wind down your conversation about issues in another person's life, offer solid solutions to the specific problems you have identified. If you can point to a reasonable way out of a predicament, the person might be more inclined to come along. At the same time, don't give the impression that you have all the answers. Make it clear that your suggestions are just a starting point, and offer to discuss any ideas the other person has. Start with a simple "What do you think?" or "Where should we go from here?" or "What should we do now?" The more you dialogue and think creatively, the less likely people will be to stay stuck in their problem.

Come Back to Grace

Talking to others about their faults is tough work. Going and showing others they have sinned and fallen short of God's ways is by definition speaking bad news. But that should never be the focus of our words. With God's help we can bring God's Good News.

We can take a lesson from Jesus's conversation with a woman at a well in Samaria (see John 4:7–26). If ever there was someone who needed urgent tips on the difference between right and wrong, it was this woman, who had a string of five husbands in her past and was now living with a sixth man. Yet Jesus didn't hammer away at her sinful lifestyle. He spent most of his time engaging her in a conversation about salvation, eternal life, true worship, and the coming Messiah. The upshot? The woman responded eagerly to this gospel-focused approach, let down her defenses, and trusted Christ to give her a new life. We are praying that your grace-packed conversations with people will prompt the same response.

Get Help

> But if he will not listen, take one or two others along, so that "every matter may be established by the testimony of two or three witnesses."
>
> Matthew 18:16

Let's be honest. When you go and show others their faults, you won't always meet with astounding success. Not only do your opponents not always see your point, but they may retaliate with words and acts that sting worse than ever. You end up feeling like you might as well have poked a hive of bees with a stick.

That's sometimes how peacemaking works. Truth is, God might use you as his mouthpiece to grab a person's attention, but only he can penetrate a heart. The apostle Paul clearly describes the limits of your job and the greatness of what God can do even when a person is snared by sinister evil:

> The Lord's servant must not quarrel; instead, he must be kind to everyone, able to teach, not resentful. Those who

oppose him he must gently instruct, in the hope that God will grant them repentance leading them to a knowledge of the truth, and that they will come to their senses and escape from the trap of the devil, who has taken them captive to do his will.

2 Timothy 2:24–26

God calls you to do your best to communicate concern, solutions, and encouragement, but you can't force change. Only he can bring about repentance.

Don't let the difficulty of peacemaking dash your commitment to careful and prayerful preparation or to pointing out sin with the most grace-packed approach you can manage. If you get good results, fantastic! You have, like Jesus predicted, won back a sister or brother. But if your efforts to go and show meet resistance, what can you do? If the results turn out to be less than what you'd hoped for, do you pack it in?

Keeping at It

That quit-or-don't-quit question has a three-part answer.

First, God wants you to focus on faithfulness, not results. If you present your concerns using the steps he has laid out in his Word, then no matter how others respond, you have succeeded in his eyes. You have done what he asks: "You must not hate your fellow citizen in your heart. If your neighbor does something wrong, tell him about it, or you will be partly to blame. Forget about the wrong things people do to you, and do not try to get even. Love your neighbor as you love yourself. I am the LORD" (Lev. 19:17–18 NCV). When you do your part, God takes it from there. In his time your words will produce exactly the results he wants.

Second, your first attempt to solve a conflict doesn't have to be your last. You might have caught your opponent off guard with your honesty. He or she might doubt your sincerity. So your first try at restoring a sister or brother might be like planting seeds. Over the next days and weeks you can go back to see what has sprouted. In fact, the Greek verb for "go" in Matthew 18:15 (as in "go and show him his fault") implies an ongoing action, not a one-time thing. The point? If at first you don't succeed, try again. Pray. Review what you have learned from this book and try to spot any mistakes you might have made. Get advice from seasoned peacemakers. If you made a glaring error, give the other person time to think—and God time to work—and then go again. Keep trying to solve the situation one-on-one until it becomes obvious that more talk is pointless or even making your conflict worse.

Third, at some point you need to decide whether it's smarter to overlook the wrong you have suffered. (Overlooking is discussed in chapter 4.) If that choice doesn't seem appropriate, there are more steps you can take—steps that get you appropriate help that might be just what you need to solve the conflict. According to Jesus, going and showing doesn't have to be the end of your efforts.

Go Alone—Then Get Help

You already know more about your next steps than you might realize, because ever since you were little you have heard labels for people who bypass the right steps for addressing wrongs. Someone who complains about you to others without talking to you first is a *gossip* or *backstabber*. A peer who runs straight to a parent or a teacher is a *tattletale* or *snitch*. And anyone who gets offended and immediately cuts you off is—well, he or she gets called all kinds of names. Even people who know nothing about the Bible or God's peacemaking strategies know these relational shortcuts are wrong. We universally dislike these flawed behaviors—at least when other people do them.

Everything you have learned about peacemaking has underlined a simple fact: the Bible commands Christians to make every possible effort to resolve conflicts one-to-one. If you truly want to glorify God in everything you do—you aim to get the log out of your own eye and intend to gently restore others according to God's plan—then you start your efforts to end a clash by going straight to the person who offended you. No detours allowed except when you need advice or assistance in complicated situations or in extreme cases such as abuse. (Remember the parameters we outlined on pages 102–3.) It's how you love like Jesus, the world's supreme peacemaker. It's the path you need to walk to enter into the authentically close relationships he created you to enjoy.

But if you have done that initial one-to-one and failed to solve your clashes in private, God offers wise ways for you to get help. Two thousand years before any of us learned about tattling, Jesus laid out a plan that takes all of this into account. In Matthew 18:15–17 he details your next moves: After talking one-on-one, you take others along. If that also fails, you appeal to the church or other authority. If none of these tactics brings about reconciliation, then you can take a time-out from the relationship. Read for yourself exactly what Jesus says:

> If your brother sins against you, go and show him his fault, just between the two of you. If he listens to you, you have won your brother over. But if he will not listen, take one or two others along, so that "every matter may be established by the testimony of two or three witnesses." If he refuses to listen to them, tell it to the church; and if he refuses to listen even to the church, treat him as you would a pagan or a tax collector.
>
> Matthew 18:15–17

The key point taught here is this: you should try to keep the circle of people involved in a conflict *as small as possible for as long as possible.* If you can solve a clash personally and privately, do it. If you run into trouble, grow the circle only as much as you need to in order to help your offender repent and get right with God and others.

As you move along in this process, your motives don't change. You are still trying to "gently restore" the person. In other words, you don't shift from showing grace to ganging up on a stubborn sinner. You simply change your tactics to get the result you have worked to accomplish all along: bringing a wrongdoer back from a dangerous place (see James 5:19–20).

Matthew 18 in Action

We can see how all this might play out with a straightforward illustration. Suppose you have a large backyard trampoline. One day a friend stops by for an impromptu jumping session. He pulls out a skateboard deck—no trucks or wheels, just the platform. Securely attached to the deck top with at least a roll of duct tape are an old pair of basketball shoes. This friend—we'll call him Matt—tosses the board onto the tramp, climbs up, and starts to lace in.

"I'm not sure that's a good idea," you mumble. Within seconds Matt is bouncing higher than even you, the tramp master, would dare. When the board blurs as he easily whips around in multiple spins, you laugh. You stop worrying about Matt's safety and start wondering when you can get a turn. Just as Matt looks like he's wearing out and will finally take a break, he pops one last huge jump and comes down with the board vertical. The skateboard deck hits the tramp nose first. Instead of flinging back skyward, Matt just stops, the board's nose slicing the tramp fabric and opening a gash more than a foot long.

The fun is over. As you stare speechlessly at the ruined tramp, Matt kicks off the board and scurries off the tramp, mumbling good-bye and heading home, leaving you alone to face your parents. They point out that you neglected your responsibility to safeguard what your friend did on the tramp. When they study the damage, they inform you that replacing the ripped fabric will run several hundred dollars. It's not fair to your siblings, they say, to let the tramp stay ruined. It's your job, they add, to come up with the cash.

Your job? You didn't gore the tramp. Any way you look at it, Matt should take sole responsibility for the tear. Wrecking the tramp might have been an accident, but there was nothing unintentional about climbing on the tramp while laced to a skateboard.

You find yourself staring at a major bill you don't think you deserve to pay. So what should you do?

Step One: Overlook Minor Wrongs

You already know your first option. Even if you think Matt is a hundred and ten percent to blame, nothing says you have to hunt him down and force him to pay up. As you mull over how you can use this situation as an opportunity to glorify God, you might conclude that your best option is to end the issue right now and drop any claims against Matt, overlooking his wrong. Why? As you simmer down, you might decide that what he did wasn't such a big deal. Accidents happen. If your roles were reversed, you would hope he would cut you some slack. You might decide you bear part of the blame for not doing more to stop Matt. Or for laughing as he continued to catch air. Or for whining as you itched for a turn. Whatever you choose to do, you need to ponder whether you have a log to extract from your own eye before you try to correct your friend.

Step Two: Talk in Private

You know the next step as well. Let's say you decide that a ripped tramp worth hundreds of dollars is too serious to let go, not to mention that you still feel mad about the heat you took from your family for something you didn't do.

After what happened, Matt might not show his face at your house anytime soon. It's your job to go to him and show him his fault, making every effort both to solve the personal issues between you and to settle up on the cash. Maybe you first get some advice from godly Christians, who can help you own your share of the problem and figure out how to best approach Matt. As you talk with him, you might end up suggesting that you split the cost of repairing the tramp.

If you and Matt don't settle the situation right away, you do your best to keep communicating with your friend. But suppose Matt doesn't come around to your viewpoint at all and refuses even to meet you halfway in sharing the blame and splitting the repair cost. If continuing to go and show privately fails and you still think the issue is too serious to overlook, you can step into the next phase of the Matthew 18 process.

Step Three: Take Along One or Two Others

Here's where you need the fresh ideas Jesus offers. When you still can't solve a clash in private, Jesus tells you to ask other people to get involved. Your goal isn't to grab your biggest friends and go rough up a wrongdoer. You bring in others to get at the facts. That's what Jesus meant in Matthew 18:16 when he quoted Deuteronomy 19:15, that "every matter" should be "established by the testimony of two or three witnesses."

Serving as "witnesses" doesn't require that people actually saw the situation firsthand, though that might be the case. That really isn't what their role is all about. The main purpose of bringing witnesses into the discussion is to get calm, Christ-centered people in the room as you meet again with Matt.

These helpers or "reconcilers" accomplish several things. Their biggest job is to help you and your opponent make your own decisions about how to restore peace. At first they might just keep your conversation moving by prompting you and Matt to really hear each other by using the listening and communication skills we have outlined. They can help get at the facts by asking questions or summing up what they hear, or they might send you looking for more details, like finding out alternatives for fixing the tramp. These reconcilers can also give personal insights on the problem. They might prod you or Matt to repent and confess by pointing out any words or acts that haven't measured up to Scripture.

In the end you and your opponent might want your reconcilers to resolve a deadlock. Wise reconcilers make sure you have made every effort to reach your own solution before they give their opinion. But you might reach a point where you and Matt agree to live by what the reconcilers determine is the best way to solve the problem.

We hope you can see that reconciling is important work, a job for wise people. Bringing others into your dispute doesn't entail grabbing a couple flighty friends to inject whatever pops into their heads. They can be peers, but whoever you pick needs to be qualified to help with communication and offer insight in line with the Bible, either specific verses or thoughts in line with the spirit of Scripture. As mad as you might be, you need to choose people you trust to stand in the middle of your dispute, not simply to take your side. Your conversations will come to a quick halt if you just pick people who agree with your point of view. You might as well be up-front and say, "I couldn't make you submit by myself, so I'm bringing people who've got my back."

Matt or any other opponent needs to be convinced that the reconcilers are real helpers who aim to be objective. After all, they aren't just *your* helpers; they are also his. They might be people you both know and trust. Before you invite others into your conversation, give Matt a heads-up by telling him what you want to do—that you think you need to involve others to help reach a solution. If Matt balks at that idea, explain the benefits. If Matt is a Christian, mention the biblical basis for this step. If he still resists, tell him you are still going to go ahead with your plan, a move that in itself might prod him to settle your dispute one-to-one.

By the way, the best way to ensure success in bringing others into the discussion is to decide with Matt or any opponent who your helpers should be. If the other person isn't in the mood for that discussion, you pick. But choose well. Don't ever give the reconcilers all the details of the dispute—your own version of all the details of the dispute, that is. Just outline the issue and tell them you need their help.

Step Four: Tell It to the Church (or Other Authority)

Do you remember feeling that little-kid urge to go tell a grown-up every time someone hurt you? Involving an authority figure in your conflict is a valid tactic. What makes it right or wrong is your timing. Only after you have considered overlooking the problem, tried to solve it yourself, and gotten the help of others do you run to the people who rule your world.

Suppose you and Matt have done your best to work with reconcilers, but you are still stuck. Or maybe Matt totally refused your plea to sit down with wise helpers. If that is where you are, Jesus laid out your next step: "Take one or two others along. . . . If he refuses to listen to them, tell it to the church" (Matt. 18:16–17).

When Jesus said to explain your situation "to the church," he didn't mean you ask your pastor for a few minutes during the worship service so you can make an announcement. Everyone doesn't need to hear all the juicy news about you or anyone else. He meant that when you are in a dispute with another Christian, you can appeal to church leadership for assistance in getting justice and peace. In dealing with a non-Christian, you can apply this principle by going to the appropriate authority figure. If a dispute happens at school, for example, you would go to a teacher, counselor, or principal.

If that sounds intense, it is. You are saying that this conflict is big enough to need the attention of your higher-ups, whoever they might be. You are staking your reputation on your willingness to abide by the decision of those in authority over you, because you can't go asking for help and then disregard what they decide. Your church or other authorities will step in with the same kind of help as the reconcilers in the last step, but their decisions are much more weighty—even mandatory. In the case of a church getting involved in a dispute between Christians, Scripture intends for the input of church leadership to be binding on both believers. In a school or work setting, your authority figures probably won't expect any less.

So you have to ask yourself whether you are ready to escalate your issue to that level. In the case of Matt and the messed-up tramp, you have to weigh a few hundred dollars (yes, that is a lot of money) against the cost of pushing the issue upward.

Still stuck? Go to step five.

Step Five: Treat the Offender as a Nonbeliever (or Take a Time-Out)

Jesus said, "Tell it to the church; and if he refuses to listen even to the church, treat him as you would a pagan or a tax collector" (Matt. 18:17). So what does that mean?

As you study Scripture you can't miss God's call for his people to act justly, seek peace, and just plain get along with others. If a Christian refuses to do these things, he is violating God's will. If he refuses to listen to his church's counsel to ditch sin and do right, Jesus says the church should "treat him *as you would* a pagan or a tax collector" (Matt. 18:17, emphasis added). Only God knows whether someone is a Christian or not. But sometimes the church needs to decide that an offender isn't living like one. Believers can't pretend that a person is doing right while he disrespects God and his people. So the church is to treat that person as if he isn't a Christian. That might mean asking someone to step down

from leadership or, in severe cases, revoking his membership. It doesn't mean that you are rude to him or suddenly
slam the door in his face. It means that you treat him like
someone who does not yet know Jesus.

For example, no one is going to kick Matt out of church
because he ruined your trampoline, but if leaders from church
went and talked to him and he stubbornly refused to follow
their advice, they might decide he is so tripped up by the sin
of pride that he should step down from teaching a student
Bible study or playing in the church band. They might follow
Matthew 5:23–24 and ask him not to take communion until he
has reconciled with you. If over a period of weeks or months
he persists in refusing to listen to their advice or do what is
right, they might conclude that he is acting so much like a non-
Christian that they would revoke his church membership. Even
then, they would keep looking for every opportunity to share
the gospel with Matt, praying for him, urging him to repent of
his sin, and inviting him to come back to the church.

None of this is for you to decide. It's up to the congregation's
leadership. And none of this is done to be mean. Like every
other step in the process Jesus laid out, the goal is to bring a
person back in line with God's will and help him reconnect with
both God and people. This is the last step in helping someone
see his sin, and the real meanness would be to let him continue
in his hurtful behavior. As Dietrich Bonhoeffer writes, "Nothing
is so cruel as the tenderness that consigns another to his sin.
Nothing can be more compassionate than the severe rebuke
that calls a brother back from the path of sin."[1]

This principle has a really practical and personal applica-
tion. When you have done all that Jesus has commanded and
still not resolved a clash, then it can be necessary to take a
time-out from your relationship. You might choose to set up
a boundary that says, "I'm not going to stay close to someone
who keeps hurting me." That step is obvious when you suffer
severe wrongs, but it's something that can be wise whenever
you have exhausted all your other options. In the case of

Matt, maybe you and your parents decide he isn't allowed on the tramp. Or you might decide not to hang out alone with him. If that's the case, tell Matt straight up what is going on and why. Keep praying for him and loving him in every way possible, and in time he might come around.

Be careful that you don't become one of those people who cuts off others over every petty offense. But a time-out can be a practical way to live out Romans 12:18: "If it is possible, as far as it depends on you, live at peace with everyone."

A Culture of Peace

Your life is filled with conflicts both more and less serious than this make-believe run-in with Matt. But the principles reach into every clash imaginable. Here's the interesting part: you and your Christian friends—maybe far more easily than a group of adults—can create a community that lives by these principles, working hard to love each other even to the extent that you call each other out when you sin. The Bible teaches that God views accountability and discipline as acts of love. It's how he brings back his wandering sheep and protects his people from being led into sin.

You might find the idea of going and showing really challenging. The thought of taking any of these next steps might feel even tougher. But think about this analogy: When a patient has cancer, it's not easy for his doctor to tell him, because the truth is painful to hear and the road ahead is very difficult. Even so, any doctor who diagnoses cancer but fails to report it to a patient would be guilty of nothing less than malpractice. After all, a patient will not have the benefit of treatment if no one tells him he has cancer.

Sin works in the same way. Left undiagnosed and untreated, it causes increasing grief. Are you willing to be a peacemaker and help others find the healing they desperately need?

G4:
GO AND BE
RECONCILED

First go and be reconciled to your brother; then come and offer your gift.

Matthew 5:24

ours after being picked up by the police, Maggie was released to her parents. Seated across the kitchen table from them, the usually poised high school junior felt like she was being interrogated all over again. Her dad sat silent while her mom prodded her with questions. Maggie recounted what had happened earlier that evening. She was in the backseat of an acquaintance's car when it was pulled over by the police. The officer accused the driver, Samantha, of being under the influence. He gave everyone a breath test. He searched the car. A police dog sniffed out a bag of marijuana in the glove compartment.

Maggie's dad finally asked a question: did Maggie know that Samantha used?

Maggie's answer was vague. "I wasn't sure."

Hearing that, Maggie's dad exploded. He couldn't understand how a smart and talented girl like Maggie could be stupid enough to ride in a car if there was even a *hint* someone might be using illegal drugs. He asked her where her sense had gone and whether she had forgotten everything she had learned at home and church. He predicted that she could forget about the good reputation she had taken years to build with her teachers and coaches and friends. People would assume Maggie had taken part in whatever Samantha had done. Most of all, he said, Maggie had broken her parents' trust, and it would be a long time before she fully got it back.

Over the next weeks, as Maggie relived in her mind every moment of what had happened that night, she recognized that she had shown awful judgment by riding with someone she didn't know well—and what little she did know about Samantha wasn't exactly good. She worried that her parents—no, make that her *dad*—suspected she was involved with the marijuana. The only times she had been out of the house since that night were to go to school, play practice, and church.

Maggie watched as her dad smoldered with anger. No matter what she said, he hardly spoke back. When he did, it was with a gruffness she rarely saw in him. The only other time in her life she had seen him like this was in the middle of a conflict in his business when a partner split from the company, taking several key clients with him. Her dad could barely say the name of the guy who had been his best friend for years.

You know that messing up big usually means you are on the receiving end of some tough love. If you use the family computer to surf pornographic sites, you can count on losing screen time and getting it back only when your parents find a way to keep you safe and steady. If you get into trouble with friends, your privileges of coming and going might look like you're in third grade. You may get grounded, or your parents will expect to sign off on the tiniest details of who you hang out with, where you go, and when you can be away from home. They might even insist on one of them or another parent tagging along wherever you go.

But dealing out consequences and setting boundaries is far different from holding a grudge or allowing an offense to wreck a relationship by refusing to forgive. Maggie needs to be forgiven. Maggie's dad needs to give forgiveness. Really give it.

If you quizzed Maggie's dad, he would say he has forgiven his cherished daughter. He's even told her so. Nevertheless, an almost impenetrable wall has grown up between them. Just at the moment when Maggie needs to reconnect with both her mom and dad, to sense their love, and to draw on their wisdom, her dad continues to hold her at a distance. Perhaps not purposely, maybe not even consciously. But anyone can see the strained relationship. Whatever he might say, he hasn't forgiven in the way God wants.

Those strained feelings don't go away automatically. A conflict still isn't fully resolved by the peacemaking steps we have covered so far. The relationship can still feel broken. Even after you have chosen to live for God's glory, gotten the log out of your own eye, and mustered courage to go firsthand to a person who has offended you . . . you still have some important work to do. As much as you might feel relieved when you have convinced others of their faults, that isn't the last step in peacemaking. You need to go and be reconciled, experiencing full relationship repair by extending forgiveness, finding a fair resolution to your clash, and working hard to overcome evil with good.

For many people, the need to give forgiveness is the point where a broken relationship stays stuck. They follow God's plan for resolving conflict right up to this point, but they get here and halt.

Like Maggie's dad, some people fear that forgiving means acting like the situation never happened. (But it still occurred. Forgiveness doesn't erase the past.) Or that forgiveness says that what an offender did was okay. (If it was okay, then the hurtful act wouldn't require forgiveness. The need to forgive proves that it was wrong!) Or that forgiveness grants a person permission to go and sin again. (If that were true, we would be highly foolish to forgive. What forgiveness does is give everyone involved in a clash a fresh start. Not a chance to do wrong but a chance to go and do right.) And some people confuse forgiveness with having warm and fuzzy feelings toward an offender. (Actually, forgiveness is a choice of the will made with the help of God. It's absolutely different from how you feel about a person or situation, although failing to forgive inevitably leads to continued hurt.)

Forgiveness doesn't fix everything that has gone wrong in a relationship. A complicated dispute takes many hours of talking, studying, praying, evaluating, and negotiating to fully solve. But forgiveness is like a doorway that gets you back to the best relationship possible. If you don't walk through it, you never exit the dimly lit room of anger, grudges, and bitterness. And that's not somewhere you want to stay.

Solid Forgiveness

Bear with each other and forgive whatever grievances you may have against one another. Forgive as
the Lord forgave you.

Colossians 3:13

Christians are the most forgiven people in the world. So we
should be the best at dishing it out—forgiveness, that is. As
soon as someone wrongs us, however, we find out as fast as
anyone just how tough it can be to forgive authentically and
completely. We might catch ourselves doling out a grudging
forgiveness that misses much of what the Bible says about
the real thing. Like Maggie's dad, we might forgive—sort
of. Our words might claim we no longer hold people's sins
against them, but our actions communicate that we want to
stay far from people who hurt us. We forgive on the outside,
all the while continuing to burn on the inside. That kind of
forgiveness can never bring about real relationship repair.

Suppose you have battled with a friend and decide to give
a small gift as a sign of a fresh start in your relationship. Yet

you show up with a present that your mother picked out, paid for, and wrapped. When your friend figures out that your mom not only forged your signature on the card but also penned the sweet note, you have done nothing to help your friendship back to health.

That's how it is when we don't forgive fully. Cheap. Fake. Even less than halfhearted and halfway. The Bible has a far higher standard, an expectation as solid as God's own character. The apostle Paul described it to his good friends in the city of Ephesus like this: "Be kind and compassionate to one another, forgiving each other, *just as in Christ God forgave you*" (Eph. 4:32, emphasis added). Paul thought the point was important enough that he echoed those words to believers in Colosse: "Forgive as the Lord forgave you" (Col. 3:13).

As Christians, we can't afford to miss the connection between God's forgiveness and our forgiveness. Because we get abundant mercy from God, he expects us to gladly pass along that mercy to others. If we count on God to generously forgive us, then we should shower others with the same generosity. You can spot that thought in the prayer Jesus himself taught us, "Forgive us our debts, as we also have forgiven our debtors" (Matt. 6:12).

You Can't Do It Alone

Imagine what would happen if God treated us like we humans tend to treat others. He might end up saying, "Well, I forgive you. But from now on I'm going to keep my distance." That wouldn't leave us feeling very forgiven.

God does far better, so forgiving like God forgives is an incredibly high standard to live up to. Fortunately, God doesn't just snap the command and leave us on our own. He gives us everything we need to imitate him.

It's impossible to truly forgive others relying solely on our own strength, especially when people have wounded us deeply or betrayed our trust. We can attempt to banish bad memories, stuff hurt feelings deep inside, and put on a faux smile every time we meet. But all the memories and feelings of hurt continue to ooze beneath the surface, poisoning our thoughts, words, and actions—that is, unless we allow God to cleanse and heal our hearts. Without his help, we won't ever really rebuild our relationships.

What exactly does it mean to try to forgive "in our own strength"? It's thinking that we can do what God does without his help. It's assuming we have power to forgive others without first building a habit of getting God's forgiveness for our own failings. It's overestimating our human ability to get over wrongs done to us. It's working hard to improve our thoughts, feelings, and actions without asking God to change us.

There is no better way to break through these barriers than to talk to God about it. We can admit that we can't forgive someone without the Lord's help and that we desperately need him to come in and change our hearts. At times I (Ken) have prayed honestly,

> God, I can't forgive _____ in my own strength. I don't want to forgive him, at least not until I make him suffer for what he did to me. He doesn't deserve to get off easy. Everything in me wants to hold it against him and keep a high wall between us so he can never hurt me again. But your Word warns me that unforgiveness will eat away at my heart and put a wall between you and me. Besides that, you have shown me that you made the supreme sacrifice in order to forgive me: giving up your own Son. Lord, help me to want to forgive. Please change my heart so that I don't want to hold this grudge. Change me so that I can forgive and love him the way you have forgiven and loved me.

This kind of bare openness and dependence on God is the first step on the path of forgiveness. God is more than happy to answer that call for help. And when we receive and rely on his grace to us, we can pass along that same grace-filled forgiveness to others.

Draw on God's Strength

When we experience God's grace toward our own sins, we can forgive even the most painful offenses. Instead of skimping on grace toward others, we start to imitate God, who puts no limits on his forgiveness toward us. We banish from our vocabulary phrases like "I could never forgive someone for _____."

Corrie ten Boom was a Dutch watchmaker's daughter. She was imprisoned with her family for aiding Jews during the Holocaust. Her elderly father and beloved sister, Betsie, died as a result of the brutal treatment they received in Nazi concentration camps. God kept Corrie alive through her imprisonment, and after World War II she traveled the globe teaching about God's enormous love. Read what she wrote in *The Hiding Place* about something that happened to her in Germany after the war:

> It was at a church service in Munich that I saw him, the former S.S. man who had stood guard at the shower room door in the processing center at Ravensbruck [a notorious Nazi concentration camp]. He was the first of our actual jailers that I had seen since that time. And suddenly it was all there—the roomful of mocking men, the heaps of clothing, Betsie's pain-blanched face.
>
> He came up to me as the church was emptying, beaming and bowing. "How grateful I am for your message, Fraulein," he said. "To think that, as you say, he has washed my sins away!"
>
> His hand was thrust out to shake mine. And I, who had preached so often to the people in Bloemendall about the need to forgive, kept my hand at my side.
>
> Even as the angry, vengeful thoughts boiled through me, I saw the sin of them. Jesus Christ had died for this man;

was I going to ask for more? "Lord Jesus," I prayed, "forgive me and help me to forgive him."

I tried to smile, I struggled to raise my hand. I could not. I felt nothing, not the slightest spark of warmth or charity. And so again I breathed a silent prayer. "Jesus, I cannot forgive him. Give me Your forgiveness."

As I took his hand the most incredible thing happened. From my shoulder along my arm and through my hand a current seemed to pass from me to him, while into my heart sprang a love for this stranger that almost overwhelmed me.

So I discovered that it is not on our forgiveness any more than on our goodness that the world's healing hinges, but on him. When he tells us to love our enemies, he gives, along with the command, the love itself.[1]

Most people in the Western world have not suffered the magnitude of wrongs that Corrie ten Boom and her family endured, and I (Ken) think often of her honest struggle and amazing reliance on God's power to forgive. Her experience with her enemy demonstrates one clear fact: because no sin is ever beyond the reach of Christ's death, no sin done against us can ever be beyond our forgiving.

What Forgiveness Isn't

Many of our objections to forgiveness come from not understanding what forgiveness is—and isn't.

We might assume forgiveness is a feeling. It isn't. It's an act of the will involving some decisions, starting with a choice to ask God to change our hearts. As he works inside us, we make another decision. We choose not to think or talk about what someone has done to hurt us. It's important to note that while God calls us to make these decisions no matter what our feelings are, these bold decisions can lead to significant changes in how we feel.

Forgiveness also isn't forgetting. Forgetting is *passive*. It counts on the hurt fading from memory simply because hours, days, months, or years have passed. Forgiving is *active*, going after the problem with a conscious choice and deliberate action. Ponder this: when God says that he "remembers your sins no more" (Isa. 43:25), he isn't saying that he can't remember our sins. He is promising that he *won't* remember them. When God forgives, he chooses to never again mull over or mention our sins. When we forgive, we rely on God's grace and consciously decide not to think or talk about what others have done to us. This can require an almost continuous effort, especially when an offense is still fresh. Fortunately, when we choose to forgive and stop focusing on an offense, our pain often eases. Once Corrie ten Boom made a decision to forgive, for example, her surge of pain instantly gave way to compassion for her former tormentor.

Finally, forgiveness isn't excusing bad behavior. Excusing says, "What you did is okay," or, "What you did wasn't really wrong," or, "You couldn't help it." Forgiveness couldn't be more different. The fact that someone needs forgiveness means that what he or she did, big or small, was so wrong that Jesus had to die for it. Forgiveness says, *We both know that what you did was wrong. But since God has forgiven me, I forgive you.* Forgiveness is really the only honest way to deal with sin. It calls wrongdoing what it is, opening the way to a solution like no amount of excusing ever can.

Think of a time you had difficulty truly forgiving another person, trouble getting to the point where you let go of an offense and refused to ever hold it against your offender. What held you back? Maybe you were waiting for a gush of warm feelings. Or you didn't realize that forgiveness works powerfully to cool inflamed emotions and calm bad memories. Or you might have thought that forgiveness would give someone permission to hurt you again and again. Those are all common reactions, but they don't catch what forgiveness really is.

What Forgiveness Is

There is an old joke about a woman who goes to her pastor for advice on improving her marriage. When the pastor asks her to sum up her greatest complaint, she replies, "Every time we get into a fight, my husband gets historical." Her pastor corrects her, saying, "You mean *hysterical*." She responds, "I mean *historical*. He keeps a mental record of everything I've ever done wrong. And whenever he gets mad, I get a history lesson!"

Anyone can understand the biting insight in that scene. If you don't learn to truly forgive, it's like you are storing up mental clips of the wrongs that others inflict on you, then playing them back again and again. There is hardly a clearer pattern for trashing relationships and depriving people of the peace and freedom that come through authentic forgiveness.

This is one of the most important biblical concepts you can ever understand. Without God's forgiveness, it is impossible to have a relationship with God. Without forgiving, you will never have right relationships with people.

So let's define what it actually means. To forgive someone is to release a person from the punishment or penalty he or she deserves. One of the Greek words often translated as "forgive," *aphiemi*, means to "let go" or "release." It can also mean to "remit," as in being done with debts that have been paid or canceled in full. Another word for "forgive," *charizomai*, means to bestow favor freely or unconditionally.

Paying Down Debt

You can think about forgiveness like this: When someone sins, they run up a debt. Someone has to pay it. Most of this debt is owed to God; he is the one against whom all

141

wrongs are ultimately done. Even our smallest sins offend our totally pure, righteous, and loving God in ways that we can't begin to imagine. But God has already canceled that bill. He sent Jesus to pay that debt on the cross. Forgiveness is undeserved, and it can't be earned. But it's never cheap, because it was paid for by the death of Christ.

Follow that? When someone sins against you, they owe God a debt. At the same time, they owe you (see Matt. 18:23–35). You also took one on the chin, so they have another debt to pay.

Here is where you face a choice. When others sin against you, you can *take* payments on the debt. Or you can *make* payments. It's possible for you to take payments on that debt in many ways. You can withhold forgiveness, dwell on the wrong, gossip, act cold and aloof, ditch the relationship, inflict emotional pain, or lash out in revenge. Those actions might give you a warped pleasure for the moment, but in the long run they demand a high price—from you. As someone once said, "Unforgiveness is the poison we drink hoping others will die." Or "When you hold someone captive through unforgiveness, the only prisoner is you."

Taking payments is an obvious but awful way of life. Your other choice is to *make* payments on the debt, releasing others from the penalties they deserve to pay. Sometimes God will enable you to do this in one relatively quick and easy payment. You decide to forgive, and you can almost hear a *whoosh*. By God's amazing grace, the debt almost instantly departs from your heart and mind. But when you have suffered a big wrong, the sin racks up a mountain of debt. It's nearly impossible to pay it all at once. You might have to put up with the impact of the other person's sin for a long time. You might fight back painful memories or endure the consequences of damages that the other person won't or can't repair. You might need to speak gracious words again and again when you really want to attack. Or you might be forced to rely on a person you barely trust.

By now you might be getting the picture that forgiveness can be extremely costly. It can leave you feeling like your debit card is completely tapped out and your pockets or purse contain nothing but lint. So how can you make payments when you feel flat broke?

Actually, you are loaded with "cash." If you believe in Jesus, you have more than enough to make these payments. When he went to the cross, the Lord paid off the ultimate debt for your sin. He has established an abundant account of grace with your name on it. There is only one thing you need to do: draw on that grace each day. You will quickly find that the account contains not only just enough to cover your own sins, but enough to make the payments of forgiveness for anyone who wrongs you.

God always gives you plenty of grace, so you can have enough for yourself and also to give away. Don't ever think, "I don't have what it takes to forgive." Just think of that fat account that holds the limitless mercy God has given you. Access it yourself whenever you need it. Then take what you have and share it.

Your Extravagant God

This sin-as-debt thing is no mind game. It accurately reflects the extravagance of everything God has done for you and your ability to forgive the biggest wrongs done against you, as long as you continually draw on God's grace. If it sounds like forgiveness will be expensive to you, remember that forgiveness was infinitely costly to God. And he simply asks you to do for others what he has already done for you. The riches of his grace toward you are mind-boggling:

> I will forgive their wickedness and will remember their sins no more.
>
> Jeremiah 31:34

As far as the east is from the west, so far has he removed our transgressions from us.

Psalm 103:12

LORD, if you punished people for all their sins, no one would be left, Lord. But you forgive us, so you are respected.

Psalm 130:3–4 NCV

[Love] keeps no record of wrongs.

1 Corinthians 13:5

We are made right with God by placing our faith in Jesus Christ. And this is true for everyone who believes, no matter who we are.

Romans 3:22 NLT

When you repent of your sin and God forgives you, he releases you from the penalty of being separated from him forever, the worst punishment you could ever experience. He promises not to remember your sins, not to hold them against you, not to let them stand between you and him ever again.

The Four Promises of Forgiveness

When someone does something to you that is bad enough—big or small—to require forgiveness, you have an opportunity to repair that relationship. You have a chance to forgive as the Lord has forgiven you, by deciding to make four concrete promises to that person:

- "I will not dwell on this incident."
- "I will not bring up this incident again and use it against you."
- "I will not talk to others about this incident."

• "I will not let this incident stand between us or get in the way of our personal relationship."

By making and keeping these promises, you do your part to tear down the walls that have been built up between you and your offender. You promise not to mope about the problem or exact punishment by holding the person at a distance. You clear the way for your relationship to move on and grow, unhindered by bad memories of past wrongs. This is exactly what God does for us, and it's what he calls us to do for others.

Imagine if Maggie's dad had acted on those promises. Yes, Maggie made a bad choice that caught her in the wrong place at the wrong time. Sure, she had to face consequences for her actions. But by refusing to forgive Maggie, her dad let an incident come between himself and his daughter. In fact, he himself sinned by erecting a thick wall of anger. Rather than helping Maggie heal and make better choices, he hurt her further and provoked her to anger. You can easily imagine Maggie becoming bitter and rebellious if her dad's attitude and actions don't change.

When Should You Forgive?

Forgiveness doesn't always come easily, but at times it comes quickly. Sometimes a person quickly admits a wrong. Jesus taught us to forgive when another believer repents.

And as we saw earlier, you can choose to overlook minor offenses right away even if a person hasn't openly repented. This kind of spontaneous forgiveness can put a dispute behind you and save you and others from needless pain.

When an offense is too serious to let go, however, and the person who wronged you hasn't repented, you can approach forgiveness as a two-stage process. You start with *an attitude of forgiveness.* When the right time arrives, you *grant forgiveness.*

An attitude of forgiveness is unconditional, a commitment you make to God. With his help, you work hard to build a loving and merciful attitude toward someone who has offended you. You live out the first promise of forgiveness—refusing to dwell on the hurtful incident or take revenge through thought, word, or action. You pray for the other person and stay ready to put your relationship back together as soon as he or she repents. Your attitude will guard you against bitterness, even if the other person takes a long time to repent.

Granting forgiveness depends on the repentance of the offender. It's all about the other three promises of forgiveness. After a serious offense (one that can't be overlooked), it wouldn't be appropriate to make those promises until the person who hurt you has repented. Until then, you might need to keep talking with the offender about his or her sin or get others involved to solve the issue. Once the other person repents, you can forgive him or her. You can speak forgiveness using all four promises. You can close the matter forever, the same way God forgives you.

God vividly demonstrates both stages of forgiveness. When Christ died on the cross, he did it with an attitude of love and mercy toward those who put him to death. He prayed, "Father, forgive them, for they do not know what they are doing" (Luke 23:34). Right after Jesus ascended to heaven, three thousand people who heard the apostle Peter's message at Pentecost were cut to the heart when they realized they had crucified the Son of God. As they repented of their sin, God granted them forgiveness (see Acts 2:22–41).

Breaking Down Barriers

Forgiveness doesn't make consequences vanish. The Bible is full of examples of people who were forgiven by God and still faced the painful results of bad choices. Being forgiven doesn't mean, for example, that we get out of paying for property damage or that we can escape from trying to make up for emotional pain we have caused others.

Back to Maggie. Wise parents set boundaries that give their children more and bigger opportunities to demonstrate their ability to handle responsibility and freedom. If Maggie's run-in with the police was a one-time mistake, her parents might not feel compelled to impose new long-term rules. But if her action was one incident in a pattern of reckless-ness and rebellion, they are likely to set strict guidelines for her safety that let her prove her ability to manage herself. Forgiveness doesn't change that.

When you forgive someone who wounded you, you might still need to enforce some consequences. There might be bills to pay, breakage to repair, apologies to make, or com-mitments to renew. But once you forgive, it's your job to do everything you can to pursue full reconciliation. Break down the walls that have grown between you. Bridge the distance that came with the dispute.

Reconciliation means that you replace hostility with peace—separation with friendship. That is what Jesus had in mind when he said, "Go and be reconciled to your brother" (Matt. 5:24). An offender doesn't have to become your best-ever friend, but your relationship should be at least as good as it was before you clashed. You can, for example, replace critical thoughts with the best possible things you can think about the person. Swap out hurtful conversations for words that heal. Get rid of antagonistic actions and show some love, even if you have to start in tiny ways. Like C. S. Lewis wrote, "Don't waste time bothering whether you 'love' your neighbor; act as if you did. As soon as we do this we find one of the great secrets. When you are behaving as if you loved someone, you will presently come to love him."[2]

When you apply this "replacement principle," you will find that your relationship has truly begun to change. It's what reconciliation is all about. By thought, words, and actions, you can demonstrate forgiveness and rebuild relationships— even with people who have badly burned you. No matter how painful the offense, with God's help, you can imitate the forgiveness and reconciliation Jesus demonstrated on the cross. Because of God's grace, you can forgive as the Lord forgave you.

It's Not All about You

Each of you should look not only to your own
interests, but also to the interests of others.

Philippians 2:4

Rebekka was deep in the grip of panic as she contemplated everything she had to accomplish to finish a major research paper that had been hanging over her for nearly two months. She'd been distracted throughout her classes, and she lagged behind at a cross country meet after school. As a friend's dad transported her back from the meet, she sat silent, staring out a window but mentally ticking down a list of everything she had to do once she got home. The car had barely stopped rolling when Rebekka popped the door, stepped out, and yelled thanks for the ride. She had her backpack unzipped before she hit the front step. And as she burst into the kitchen ready to go to work on the family computer . . . there sat her younger brother Derek, listening to music and instant-messaging friends.

Rebekka didn't pause. Grabbing the mouse, she clicked shut Derek's messaging program and bumped him out of his spot in front of the computer. "I need this," she snapped.

Concrete Disputes

Back at the start of this book we said that a conflict is "a difference in opinion or purpose that frustrates your goals or desires—or someone else's." Whenever you and another person are at odds over what you think, want, or do, you are experiencing conflict. Every conflict results in some kind of offense in which at least one person walks away feeling stung. So far you have discovered that by using God's strategies for addressing the problem, you can often work past these hurts and gain a relationship.

The parts of a conflict having to do with hurt and offended feelings are what we call "personal issues." But many clashes also concern "material issues," concrete points that need to be addressed before a conflict is truly resolved. Rebekka and Derek, for example, need to sort through the personal issues between them, like the hurt Rebekka caused her younger brother. They can start by Derek telling Rebekka how angry he felt when she shut down his chats and shoved him away from the screen. Once Rebekka admits her wrong, Derek can tell her that he forgives her, and they will have a repaired relationship. But there is more to ending the conflict than that. They might make up, but they still often want the computer at the same time. Something else needs to happen to resolve this issue.

Many conflicts involve issues beyond hurt feelings. While you need to repair those wrongs, you can't ignore the concrete concerns. This is true not just when it comes to who gets the computer but also in other disputes like the time of your curfew . . . how much you should get paid for a job or chore . . . who makes or misses the starting lineup . . . whose turn it is to do the dishes . . . which sibling gets the TV when multiple friends come over . . . who should fill the gas tank . . . who really ate all the cookies . . . whether a grade was fair. . . who gets the car on Friday night . . . or whether you or your parents should pay for a clothing item. The list could be endless. Material issues involve all the stuff of life, all the things big and small that we fight over at home, school, church, and elsewhere with friends and strangers alike.

In dealing with a conflict, you might reach a breakthrough where you and an offender settle your personal issues and are at peace with each other. But if the conflict concerns any material issues, the disagreement will happen again and again until you do something further. You need to take the next step and negotiate an agreement that satisfies everyone.

We want to give you solid principles to help you solve these disputes. Amazingly, these tactics work no matter who you deal with—the peers you can look at eye-to-eye, authorities over you such as parents or bosses or teachers, or people over whom you wield some amount of power or influence, like younger siblings. These principles allow you to approach anyone in your life with care and respect, allowing you to reach real solutions.

Competitive Negotiation

Many people approach a negotiation like a tug-of-war, where each side pulls all-out to get what it wants, leaving it to the other side to fend for its own needs. When one side wins in this winner-takes-all fight, the other side loses and gets dragged into a mud pit.

This competitive approach isn't always wrong. It may be appropriate when you need to hammer out immediate agreements or when you defend a key moral principle on which you find little room for compromise. But there are downsides to this way of reaching a settlement.

To begin with, being competitive is frequently a bad choice if your aim is the best possible result. When people work against each other, they tend to focus on surface issues and ignore people's deeper needs and wants. The solutions they reach seldom truly satisfy anyone, because a competitive approach carves up a situation like a pie. For one side to get more pie, the other side has to get less. There is no way for you to get the fat slice you want without forcing the other person to settle for a skinny one. This "fixed pie" attitude doesn't give you the flexibility to craft truly creative solutions.

Competitive negotiation can also be inefficient. The back-and-forth starts with each side stating its position. Progress comes with round after round of compromises and concessions. Each advance is half the size of the last but takes twice as long to get done. It's a time waster and frustration builder.

Because competitive negotiating polarizes people to opposite ends of a problem, it can significantly damage relationships. It tempts people to be highly self-centered and often offensive. Because these negotiations focus on concrete issues instead of personal perceptions, attitudes, and concerns, people get the message that their thoughts and feelings don't matter. And arguments can spin out of control into intimidation, manipulation, and attack.

Rebekka and Derek could try a competitive approach to solving their disagreement, but they likely wouldn't get very far. Even as Rebekka spouts off the extensive research she needs to do, the intense pressure she feels, and the impossible deadline she faces, Derek prepares his best arguments about being the first one to the computer, never getting screen time because Rebekka always hogs the machine, and how all of his friends are expecting him online. In a competitive approach to negotiations, this sister and brother each worry only about winning what they want. It's a tug-of-war that consumes enormous energy. It either ends in a deadlock or lands someone in the slop.

Cooperative Negotiation

You can avoid most of these problems by rejecting the attitude that says, "I'm in this for me, myself, and I." You can instead approach others with an attitude that communicates, "Let's work this out." When you aim to do *cooperative* negotiation, you commit to deliberately seek solutions that benefit everyone involved. By working with your opponents rather than against them, you are far more likely to grasp everyone's core needs and develop bigger and better solutions. When you do this right, cooperative negotiation is efficient, because you don't waste time posturing or playing games. Best of all, this style of negotiation tends to preserve or even improve relationships because you pay attention to personal concerns.

Cooperative negotiation gets high marks in the Bible, which tells us over and over to work actively for the well-being of others:

> Love your neighbor as yourself.
>
> Matthew 22:39

> [Love] is not self-seeking.
>
> 1 Corinthians 13:5

> So in everything, do to others what you would have them do to you, for this sums up the Law and the Prophets.
>
> Matthew 7:12

> Do nothing out of selfish ambition or vain conceit, but in humility consider others better than yourselves. Each of you should look not only to your own interests, but also to the interests of others.
>
> Philippians 2:3–4

By the way, love for others seldom means simply caving in to their demands. The Bible recognizes our desire and responsibility to look out for our own interests (see Phil. 2:4). Jesus actually calls us to be "as shrewd as snakes and as innocent as doves" (Matt. 10:16). That Greek word for "shrewd," *phronimos*, means to be wise in a practical way. A wise person doesn't give in to others without a good reason. He or she instead gets all the details and brainstorms creative solutions that honor God and pass on lasting benefits to as many people as possible. Sometimes that means giving way to another person's genuine needs. But it usually requires that both sides contribute to a solution.

The PAUSE Process

The best way to sum up what these Bible passages imply about cooperative negotiation is to say that the process should be jam-packed with love and wisdom—not just one or the other, but both. I (Ken) have found that living out this loving and wise approach usually requires us to take five basic steps that you can remember with this simple statement: "When you need to negotiate, PAUSE." PAUSE is an acronym that stands for the following steps:

- Prepare
- Affirm relationships
- Understand interests
- Search for creative solutions
- Evaluate options objectively and reasonably

If you carefully follow each step, you will give even bad situations a good chance of coming to a great conclusion that benefits everyone involved.

PAUSE: Prepare

You simply can't negotiate well without preparing well, especially when issues are big and feelings even bigger. Proverbs 14:22 says it like this: "Those who plan to do good will be loved and trusted" (NCV). When we say "prepare," we don't mean that you make a list of arguments guaranteed to smash your opponent. Attempt instead to look inside and out at the whole situation.

How do you do that? This is such a crucial task that there are many steps you can take.

Throughout the process you can *pray*, asking God for humility, discernment, and wisdom as you prepare. *Get the facts* by collecting all the information you can about the situation. You might talk to witnesses, do research, or even read documents like family contracts or school handbooks. You can *identify issues and interests* (more on that in a minute) by trying to figure out the real cause of the disagreement. Carefully list the issues involved, identifying both what you want and what others want, as best you understand it.

Don't forget to *study the Bible*, searching for biblical principles that can guide your actions. *Develop options* before you talk with your opponent so you can propose one or two reasonable solutions to the problem. Be prepared to explain how each option will benefit that person. Take that a step further and *anticipate reactions*, putting yourself in your adversary's shoes, predicting likely reactions and developing a response to each. *Get advice* by asking people you trust for insight into the problem. *Plan ahead* by deciding how you will start the discussion and what you will do if talking doesn't work. *Pick the right place and time* to optimize your chance for success.

You know how the dispute between Rebekka and Derek is likely to get solved in the short run. Mom or Dad will utter a decision, most likely based on homework versus social networking. You know which one wins. But picture this sister and brother backing up and trying cooperative negotiation to find a long-term solution to their dispute. Rather than engaging in a shouting match in which each tries to score points against the other, they separately take time to pray about the situation and jot down not only what they want but also what the other likely wants. Then they carry their preparation a step further and brainstorm possibilities that meet the needs of both.

Now these siblings are on track to cooperate rather than compete, finding peace instead of endless strife. They might actually solve the computer problem for themselves instead of needing repeated parental verdicts.

PAUSE: Affirm Relationships

Deep insight: conflict generally needs two basic ingredients—people and a problem. (Okay—it's pretty obvious.) Too often we ignore the feelings and concerns of people and play up the problems that separate us. It's a recipe for further insult and alienation, which hardly help solve conflicts. You can beat these needless complications by showing and speaking your respect for your offender while you are together.

Normal sister and brother that they are, Rebekka and Derek aren't about to start their negotiating session with a giant hug. But maybe they could muster words like "I appreciate having you as my brother (or sister)." Or "I want to get along with you, so I want to do whatever I can to work this out." Or "Thank you for sitting down to talk. You're good at showing me that you care."

We know that although any of those phrases might sound good, it is very difficult to say such words to a family member or friend, much less someone you don't know well. But as you work to solve any conflict, search for the best and most sincere words you can think of to communicate your thoughts and feelings of respect for the other person. Your words need to be true, of course, or you will smell hypocritical.

You can also try these methods of signaling respect: *Talk politely* by not sliding into sarcasm, sharpness, or anger. *Listen carefully* (flip back to chapter 8 for hints). *Start with personal concerns.* Instead of jumping right to material issues that separate you, get to your opponent's personal frustrations as soon as possible. *Submit to authority.* Offer your brilliant insights and be persuasive, but respect the role of people who are over you. Support their decisions as best you can. *Understand.* That's a big challenge in the middle of a disagreement. But pay attention to your offender's thoughts and feelings. Ask questions when you don't get something. *Look out for the interests of others.* Hunt for solutions that would really satisfy others' needs and wants. *Say thanks.* When someone makes a valid point or a kind move, say so. Express your appreciation.

If you authentically communicate care and deal with personal issues with a grace-filled respect, you will generally clear the way to talk through material issues honestly and effectively.

PA*USE:* Understand Interests

The apostle Paul coaches us, "Look not only to your own interests, but also to the interests of others" (Phil. 2:4). It sounds obvious, but you can't begin to do that if you don't understand what interests everyone brings to the discussion. You might have a firm grasp of your own goals, but it never hurts to spell those out in writing. It takes hard work, however, to understand an opponent's interests so well that you can put them side by side to see where you agree and where you split.

You will really start to understand this concept of interests when you catch the important difference between an *issue* (the concrete problem that needs to be addressed, best put in the form of a question), a *position* (a desired outcome or end result), and an *interest* (a concern, desire, need, limitation, or anything else that motivates people). To comprehend why those distinctions matter, you can look for them in the case of Rebekka and Derek:

- Issue: Who should get to use the family computer right now?
- Positions: Rebekka says, "Derek should get off the computer so I can finish my homework." Derek thinks, "Rebekka can wait. I was here first."

- Interests: Put simply, Rebekka wants to get her home-work done. Derek wants to connect with friends.

Here's where the ability to identify interests gets powerful. After all, it's not tough to see the *issue*. Just as easy to notice is that Rebekka and Derek's *positions* are totally incompat-ible. They are win-lose, either-or. They can't both be on the computer at the same time, at least not doing what they want to do. But their *interests*? What Rebekka and Derek want aren't necessarily at odds. If they can find reasonable solutions that let Rebekka do her homework and Derek hang with friends, then they both win. (Put a couple other ways, they can each get a fat slice of the pie. Or they can find an outcome in which neither takes a dive in the mud.)

Interests are often surprisingly compatible. Both Rebekka and Derek know they need to get homework done. They both enjoy time with friends. That common ground is a starting point. It allows them to be on the same page when asking and answering the key question in any cooperative negotiation, "How can we best satisfy both of our interests?" Or, put another way, "How could we all get what we want?" They can start to be creative rather than confrontational. If they are aware of each other's interests and each works to meet those needs, they can find a better way to share the computer both now and in the future.

As you try to negotiate toward a solution in a dispute, you need to identify the issue and understand your positions. But it's far more important to look past your positions and get at each other's interests. The more fully you grasp and look out for your opponent's interests, the more ready you are to take the next step.

PAUSE: Search for Creative Solutions

Now you can get just a little crazy. Once you understand each other's interests, you are fully ready to spontaneously invent solutions to your clash. You and your opponent should feel free to mention any idea that comes to mind. This isn't the time for evaluation and decision. In fact, your goal during this stage is to brainstorm ways to "expand the pie," to explore ideas that get you the best solution possible. As you come up with thoughts, try to sell your opponent on them. Point out the benefit each idea could bring not just to you but to him or her.

Rebekka and Derek might take time in the heat of the immediate homework crisis to search for creative solutions. For example, Rebekka might offer to spend a few minutes driving Derek to a friend's house in return for uninterrupted computer time for the rest of the evening. She might loan him her cell phone so he can chat with his friends. Once they make space for long-term discussions, they could see that their options range from signing up for computer time to splitting the cost of another used computer to a dozen other options.

When you focus on interests rather than positions, you and your opponent both put your brains to work on generating solutions that could satisfy everyone.

PAUSE: Evaluate Options Objectively and Reasonably

Not every idea is the best idea. The final step in the PAUSE strategy is to evaluate possible solutions objectively and reasonably so you can reach the most promising agreement.

You might find negotiations at this point sliding back into disagreement. Rebekka might decide she has enough worries of her own and has no reason to care about her younger brother's social connections. Derek may just demand his rights.

When disagreement hits, each side needs to commit to avoiding a battle of wills. Instead of relying on feelings and opinions, dig for objective data to help you decide what solution will really work. Rebekka might need a gentle reminder that Scripture calls her not to ignore her brother's needs, even if at the moment they seem insignificant to hers. In a discussion of how to share the computer long term, they might each do a little research, checking with friends and reporting back how other families split up screen time.

This is no time to give up and announce a one-sided "agreement." Don't quit listening. Continue to put yourself inside your opponent's head and try to see things from that perspective. Build on that person's ideas and stay open to critique of your own. Remember: you are hunting for objective evidence for which proposal will best meet everyone's interests. If you hang in there, you just might satisfy everyone in the dispute.

When a disagreement has been significant, put what you decide in writing. If you don't settle up right away, come back for another discussion. Keep treating the other person the way you want to be treated. Press on.

Hit PAUSE

Simple principles—with big results. Many conflicts contain not just personal components but also material issues that need to be resolved. The PAUSE process means that negotiating these points doesn't have to be a brutal tug-of-war. If you do this right, plenty of people will respond well. Together you can find mutually beneficial solutions to your common problems. You can even be an example to others of how to use God's principles. Sometimes all it takes to get a conflict solved is for you to remember that it's not all about you. Like Scripture says, "Look not only to your own interests, but also to the interests of others" (Phil. 2:4).

Overpower Evil
with Good

Do not be overcome by evil, but overcome evil with good.

Romans 12:21

We didn't write this book to give you a load of information that would fill up your brain and sit unused. No matter who you are or what your life is like, you face conflict at every turn. We trust that if you have read this far, you have tried some of the ideas in this book. Not just a few here and there, but each of the key points of the peacemaking process from beginning to end. We hope you have glimpsed just how practical the Four G's are for life:

G1: *Glorify God.*
How can I honor God in this situation?

G2: *Get the log out of your eye.*
How can I own my part of this conflict?

G3: *Gently restore.*
How can I help others own their contribution to this clash?

G4: *Go and be reconciled.*
How can I pass along God's forgiveness and help reach a reasonable solution?

Now there is one more piece of information you need to know: no matter how well you put God's peacemaking process into action, some conflicts will rage on.

We haven't been trying to sell you on something that doesn't work. I (Ken) have spent most of my adult life seeing how these truths have brought about relationship miracles for me and countless Christians who used them. Kevin has for many years used similar biblical strategies with youth and families in diverse settings. But we are both quick to say that solving a situation isn't just up to you or me. It takes two to start a fight, and it takes two to fully end it. The question we still need to answer is this: what do you do when your best efforts don't create peace?

If unresolved conflict wasn't such a rotten experience, we could just shake our heads and laugh at how our peacemaking can turn out. Not only do some people stay stubborn and defensive and hardened by sin, others actually become more antagonistic, inventing fresh and ingenious ways to frustrate or mistreat us. We can be on the receiving end of torment from classmates, teammates, co-workers, enemies, strangers, friends, or even the folks who share our roof. If we are honest we have to admit that we can get caught up in the same bad patterns too. Our natural human reaction is to strike back at people who continue to hurt us, or at least stop doing them any kind of good. But if peacemaking doesn't always get the results we want, think how little peacefaking and peacebreaking accomplish for us! While they might look like they solve an issue for a while, the problem is still there.

God's Better Way

You need a better plan than falling back on the creed too many live by: "Do to others before they do to you," or "Dish it out to others before they dish it out to you," or "Hit them before they hit you." As we have seen throughout this book, Jesus calls us to a radically different course of action:

> But I tell you who hear me: Love your enemies, do good to those who hate you, bless those who curse you, pray for those who mistreat you.... Then your reward will be great, and you will be sons of the Most High, because he is kind to the ungrateful and wicked. Be merciful, just as your Father is merciful.
>
> Luke 6:27–28, 35–36

Even when peace doesn't come as easily as we hope, our job is to continue to love like God does.

To most people, this approach seems downright naïve, like we are conceding defeat and letting ourselves get rolled over. The apostle Paul knew better. He had noticed that God doesn't operate the way the world does. He also understood the extreme power we have because we know Christ. Check his response when he was hit with intense, repeated personal attacks:

> For though we live in the world, we do not wage war as the world does. The weapons we fight with are not the weapons of the world. On the contrary, they have divine power to demolish strongholds. We demolish arguments and every pretension

that sets itself up against the knowledge of God, and we take captive every thought to make it obedient to Christ.

2 Corinthians 10:3–5

Paul didn't resort to the world's weapons—things like meanness, selfishness, intimidation, control, or anger. He drew power from the most life-changing news we can ever hear: through the death and resurrection of his Son, God forgave all our sins and made peace with us. If you trust Christ, he gives you the strength to ditch sin, do good, and be his ambassadors taking peace to the world (see 2 Cor. 5:16–20). He makes you able to do some amazingly strange acts, from confessing sin to talking kindly to others about their failings, from laying down rights to forgiving deep hurts—even when mistreatment goes on and on.

We want you to think of the most stubborn ongoing conflict you face right now, one that never seems to run out of burning hot steam. Then look how Romans 12:14–21 says you should act toward people who persist in opposing you:

> Bless those who persecute you; bless and do not curse. Rejoice with those who rejoice; mourn with those who mourn. Live in harmony with one another. Do not be proud, but be willing to associate with people of low position. Do not be conceited. Do not repay anyone evil for evil. Be careful to do what is right in the eyes of everybody. If it is possible, as far as it depends on you, live at peace with everyone. Do not take revenge, my friends, but leave room for God's wrath, for it is written: "It is mine to avenge; I will repay," says the Lord. On the contrary: "If your enemy is hungry, feed him; if he is thirsty, give him something to drink. In doing this, you will heap burning coals on his head." Do not be overcome by evil, but overcome evil with good.

God calls you not to flop down in front of evil but to go on a shock-and-awe offensive—not to beat up or destroy your opponents but to win them over, help them see the truth, and usher them into a right relationship with God. You can spot five principles in this passage that sum up what you should do and wrap together everything we have already told you in this book.

Control Your Tongue

The more intense the dispute, the more carefully you need to watch every word you say (see Rom. 12:14). Prolonged conflict invites you to gossip, slander, and spew reckless words, especially if your opponent is saying harsh things about you. Don't do those things. You will only make the situation worse. Make every effort to say only grace-filled words that are both true and helpful, speaking kindly about your opponent whenever possible. As Peter wrote, "Do not repay evil with evil or insult with insult, but with blessing, because to this you were called so that you may inherit a blessing" (1 Peter 3:9).

Get Godly Advice

Paul recognized how tough it is to battle evil alone. That is why he tells you to hang tight with people through the highest highs and lowest lows (see Rom. 12:15–16). Beating your head against what seems like an immovable wall of conflict is a quick path to doubting all of the biblical principles you have been learning. Get friends who encourage you to do right rather than push you toward doing wrong. Allow them to remind you of everything the Bible promises and to challenge you to obey God at all times.

Keep Doing Right

You can't escape the point of Romans 12:17, the clear command never to pay back evil for evil. That verse tells you to continue doing right even when it looks like your opponent will never cooperate. Check similar advice from Peter:

> Live such good lives among the pagans that, though they accuse you of doing wrong, they may see your good deeds and glorify God on the day he visits us. . . . For it is God's will that by doing good you should silence the ignorant talk of foolish men. . . . But do this with gentleness and respect, keeping a clear conscience, so that those who speak maliciously against your good behavior in Christ may be ashamed of their slander.
>
> 1 Peter 2:12, 15; 3:15–16

You can live in a way that sooner or later reasonable people watching your life will admit you are doing right.

Recognize Your Limits

You can choose to do right in the toughest situations, but you can't make others do the same. When you deal with difficult people, recognize that some people might totally refuse to succumb to your kindness. So Paul wrote, "If it is possible, as far as it depends on you, live at peace with everyone" (Rom. 12:18). Do everything you can to be reconciled to others, and then don't waste energy fretting if things don't work out. Look ahead, keeping one eye open to fresh opportunities to make peace. And let God deal with people his own way.

Use the Ultimate Weapon

The biggest and best way to respond to a stubborn opponent comes in Romans 12:20–21: "'If your enemy is hungry, feed him; if he is thirsty, give him something to drink. In doing this, you will heap burning coals on his head.' Do not be overcome by evil, but overcome evil with good." That is your ultimate weapon: deliberate, focused love. Those words about "burning coals" come from the practice of ancient armies using burning coals to fend off attackers. No combatant could resist this weapon for long. Love has the same overwhelming power. At the least, loving others protects you. And God might use your love to finally bring that person around. You have no chance of overcoming evil with more evil. But you can overcome evil with good.

Trouncing Evil

Need a picture of that powerful love? It's vividly described in Ernest Gordon's book *To End All Wars*. Captured by the Japanese during World War II, Gordon was forced with other British prisoners to endure years of horrible treatment while building the notorious "Railroad of Death" through Thailand. He faced the starvation and disease of the prison camps and the brutality of his captors, who killed hundreds of his comrades. But Gordon survived and became a living picture of Christian love trouncing human evil.

This love shone with incredible brightness one day when Gordon and his fellow prisoners came upon a trainload of wounded Japanese soldiers being transported to Bangkok. Here is how Gordon describes the scene:

> They were on their own and without medical care. . . . Their uniforms were encrusted with mud, blood, and excrement. Their wounds, sorely inflamed and full of pus, crawled with maggots. We could understand now why the Japanese were so cruel to their prisoners. If they didn't care for their own, why should they care for us?
>
> The wounded men looked at us forlornly as they sat with their heads resting against the carriages waiting fatalistically for death. They were the refuse of war; there was nowhere to go and no one to care for them. . . .

Without a word, most of the officers in my section un-buckled their packs, took out part of their ration and a rag or two, and, with water canteens in their hands went over to the Japanese train to help them. Our guards tried to pre-vent us . . . but we ignored them and knelt by the side of the enemy to give them food and water, to clean and bind up their wounds, to smile and say a kind word. Grateful cries of "Aragatto!" ("Thank you!") followed us when we left. . . .

I regarded my comrades with wonder. Eighteen months ago they would have joined readily in the destruction of our captors had they fallen into their hands. Now these same men were dressing the enemy's wounds. We had experienced a moment of grace, there in those blood-stained railway cars. God had broken through the barriers of our prejudice and had given us the will to obey his command, "Thou shalt love."[1]

Keep that picture in your mind when you wonder whether loving those who hurt or even hate you is worth the price. At the risk of death and in the midst of war, Gordon and his friends brought peace to their enemies in a sweltering Thai jungle.

Few people will ever suffer that kind of abuse or have to stretch across such an enormous chasm to love those who have done them wrong. But the same principles apply in your conflict, large or small. As you love even your enemies, you glorify God. You guard your own heart against death by hatred. And God might choose to use your loving acts to bring peace to the soul of your most venomous opponent.

We pray that these words of Paul will encourage you to count on God's awesome power as you work to make peace in your broken world: "So my dear brothers and sisters, stand strong. Do not let anything move you. Always give your-selves fully to the work of the Lord, because you know that your work in the Lord is never wasted" (1 Cor. 15:58 NCV). Overcome evil. Do good.

QUESTIONS FOR DISCUSSION AND REFLECTION

Introduction

1. How is conflict a positive opportunity?
2. What clashes do you regularly face? What are some conflicts you would like to resolve?
3. Why strive to be a peacemaker?

G1: Glorify God

1. When have you done the right thing and had it turn out wrong? What made the situation go bad?
2. Does being a good person help you avoid clashes? Why—or why not?
3. How does God get glory when you deal well with conflict?

Chapter 1: Your Amazing Opportunity

1. Describe the kinds of attitudes and actions that characterize the three ways people respond to conflict—peacefaking, peacebreaking, or peacemaking.

2. How do you usually respond to conflict—as a peacefaker, peacebreaker, or peacemaker? Explain what you do.
3. What exactly is conflict? Why does it happen?
4. How is conflict like a slippery slope?
5. How can clashes be good? What kind of conflicts are bad?
6. What benefits come to you and others when you solve conflict God's way?

Chapter 2: Real Peace

1. What kinds of emotions do you see in the people around you? What emotions usually rule your heart?
2. How do we know the Lord is "the God of peace"?
3. What is 3-D peace? What's so great about each dimension?
4. Why does Christian unity matter so much? What happens when Christians don't get along?
5. What does Satan have to do with conflict?
6. How hard are you willing to strive to be a peacemaker? How do you know if you're going all-out?

Chapter 3: Trust God, Do Good

1. How do you act when you clash with others? Make a list of the concrete, specific things you do.
2. What feels tough about handling conflict God's way?
3. When you find yourself in the middle of a conflict, what makes God worth trusting? What's your proof that you can count on him?
4. Who in the Bible demonstrates trust in God in spite of questions, doubts, and fears? Details, please.
5. What real-life, right-now person do you know who exhibits amazing trust in God?
6. Why do you need trust to be God's go-anywhere, do-any-thing, follow-no-matter-what kind of person? How much do you have that kind of trust—or not?

G2: Get the Log Out of Your Eye

1. What does it mean to "get the log out of your own eye"?
2. Is it ever okay to point out the failings of others? Explain.
3. What two kinds of faults are we likely to show in a conflict?

Chapter 4: Get Over It

1. How do you feel when others put you under a microscope, scrutinizing and criticizing your every move?
2. What does the Bible tell you about overlooking an offense—good idea or bad idea?
3. Is overlooking a cop-out? Explain your answer.
4. How do you know when overlooking isn't the right choice?
5. Think of a conflict you often face—and picture yourself overlooking your opponent's faults. How do you feel about that?
6. When is it right to surrender your rights? When is it wrong?

Chapter 5: The State of Your Heart

1. What was the last major conflict you experienced? What wants and desires inside of you contributed to the conflict?
2. When have you had a good desire that went bad—wanting a right thing at the wrong time, in the wrong way, and in the wrong amount?
3. What is idolatry?
4. How can you tell if a good desire has crossed the line into sin?
5. Explain what this means: "I desire . . . I demand . . . I judge . . . I punish." What behaviors go along with each?
6. What's the one cure for an idolatrous heart? Why does that work?

Chapter 6: Breaking Loose

1. What is grace? What does it have to do with peacemaking?
2. Explain what repentance is—and isn't.

3. What happens when you refuse to confess your sins?
4. How can you spot sin in your life? Why bother?
5. As you read the Scriptures in this chapter, what sins came to mind? What are you going to do about them?
6. What are the "Seven A's" of confession? How are they beneficial?

G3: Gently Restore

1. What's tough about stepping in to help when others sin?
2. When should you get involved—and when should you butt out?
3. What does it look like when you *katartizo* the people in your world?

Chapter 7: Just between Us

1. When have you tried to confront others about their sins? How did it turn out?
2. How should you "go and show" others their faults? How is what Jesus prescribes in Matthew 18 different from simply getting in the face of others?
3. How do you know if a sin is too serious to overlook?
4. What attitudes and actions disqualify you from helping others see their sins?
5. In what situations is it a bad or dangerous idea to go straight to an offender?
6. What good things can result if you go and point out the faults of others?

Chapter 8: Speak Truth—but Listen First

1. How might your words help or hurt the situation when you go and show others their faults?
2. What can you do to prepare yourself before you talk with others about their failings?

3. Think of a conflict you face right now. What would be the best time, place, and method to deal with it?
4. How is communicating with others about their faults more than simply confronting?
5. What important pointers can you put into practice as you go to others?
6. How can you inject grace into your conversations with others?

Chapter 9: Get Help

1. What's your next step when you go in person to show someone his or her sin and that person doesn't listen?
2. How might that tactic help a situation? What are you trying to accomplish?
3. What cost to you does this next step involve? How do you know whether it's the right step to take?
4. What relational shortcuts do we sometimes take in place of this next step? Which are you most likely to do?
5. What can you do if bringing other witnesses doesn't help? And what comes after that?
6. Suppose your opponent doesn't respond at all to your efforts. Why keep working at this process?

G4: Go and Be Reconciled

1. What is reconciliation? Why do we need it?
2. Describe what reconciliation looks like in real life.
3. Explain what forgiveness is—and isn't.

Chapter 10: Solid Forgiveness

1. Why should Christians be great at forgiving?
2. What is "fake forgiveness"? How does it differ from the real thing?
3. Where do you get the ability to forgive? How do you get it?

4. How have you seen forgiveness in real life? What about it looks appealing—or unappealing?
5. What are the four promises of forgiveness? What good do they do?
6. When should you forgive?

Chapter 11: It's Not All about You

1. What's the difference between a "personal issue" and a "material issue"?
2. Give an example of a material issue you face.
3. What's the best way to approach negotiation? Why look out for the interests of others?
4. How can you watch out for the interests of others without caving in to their demands?
5. Sum up each step of the PAUSE process in your own words.
6. What's the ultimate goal of this hard work of negotiation?

Chapter 12: Overpower Evil with Good

1. Does peacemaking solve every conflict? Why—or why not?
2. What can you do when peacemaking doesn't get the results you hoped for?
3. How is continuing to love people not the same as giving up?
4. Name some practical actions you can take toward your opponents who keep behaving badly.
5. How is love your ultimate weapon? What can it accomplish?
6. How do you know that your obedience to God is never wasted?

NOTES

Chapter 1: Your Amazing Opportunity

1. U.S. Centers for Disease Control and Prevention, "Suicide Trends among Youths and Young Adults Aged 10–24 Years—United States, 1990–2004," *Morbidity and Mortality Weekly Report*, September 7, 2007. http://www.cdc.gov/MMWR/preview/mmwrhtml/mm5635a2.htm.

Chapter 5: The State of Your Heart

1. F. Samuel Janzow, *Luther's Large Catechism: A Contemporary Translation with Study Questions* (St. Louis: Concordia, 1978), 13.

Chapter 6: Breaking Loose

1. R. C. Sproul, *The Intimate Marriage* (Wheaton: Tyndale, 1988), 32.

Chapter 9: Get Help

1. Dietrich Bonhoeffer, *Life Together*, trans. John W. Doberstein (New York: Harper & Row, 1954), 107.

Chapter 10: Solid Forgiveness

1. Corrie ten Boom, *The Hiding Place* (New York: Bantam, 1974), 238.
2. C. S. Lewis, *Mere Christianity* (New York: Macmillan, 1960), 116.

Chapter 12: Overpower Evil with Good

1. Ernest Gordon, *To End All Wars* (Grand Rapids: Zondervan, 2002), 197–98.

Ken Sande is president of Peacemaker Ministries and author of the bestselling book *The Peacemaker*. He has conciliated hundreds of family, business, and church disputes and serves frequently as a consultant to pastors and other leaders as they work to resolve conflicts. Sande speaks throughout the world on biblical peacemaking. He and his wife, Corlette, and their two teenagers live in Billings, Montana.

Kevin Johnson is the bestselling author or coauthor of more than forty books for kids and teens. He now brings his diverse youth ministry experience to his role as a discipleship pastor and leader of Journey, a next-generation worship community in Minneapolis, Minnesota, where he lives with his wife, Lyn, and their three children.